Sidney Crosby

A HOCKEY STORY

PAUL ARSENEAULT
WITH PAUL HOLLINGSWORTH

SECOND EDITION

NIMBUS
PUBLISHING

Nimbus Publishing Limited
PO Box 9166, Halifax, NS B3K 5M8
(902) 455-4286   www.nimbus.ns.ca

Printed and bound in Canada

Paul Arseneault photo: Flo Guitard
Paul Hollingsworth photo: Steve Townsend/CTV Atlantic

Library and Archives Canada Cataloguing in Publication

Arseneault, Paul, 1963-
Sidney Crosby : a hockey story / Paul Arseneault ; with
Paul Hollingsworth.
ISBN 978-1-55109-664-3

1. Crosby, Sidney, 1987-. 2. Hockey players—Canada—
Biography.   I. Hollingsworth, Paul, 1969- II. Title.

GV848.5.C76A78 2008   796.962092
C2008-901460-X

NOVA SCOTIA
Tourism, Culture and Heritage

We acknowledge the financial support of the Government
of Canada through the Book Publishing Industry Development Program (BPIDP) and the Canada Council, and of
the Province of Nova Scotia through the Department of
Tourism, Culture and Heritage for our publishing activities.

This book is dedicated to the memory of my father, Arthur, and my brother Kenneth.

—Paul Arseneault

Table of Contents

VII   **Foreword**

1   **Introduction**

7   **Chapter 1** – The Odyssey Begins

9   **Chapter 2** – Unbeatable in Bathurst: The 2002 Air Canada Cup

15   **Chapter 3** – Young Man Goes West

21   **Chapter 4** – Sidney Franchise: The Arrival of Number 87 to the Q

33   **Chapter 5** – Learning to Lead: The 2004 and 2005 World Junior Championships

43   **Chapter 6** – Lessons in Defeat: The 2005 Memorial Cup

55   **Chapter 7** – The Rookie

65   **Chapter 8** – Sophomore Season

75   **Chapter 9** – Chasing Destiny

79   **Photo Credits**

80   **About the Authors**

First it was number 99, then it was number 66...now the hottest number in professional hockey belongs to Sidney Crosby, number 87 of the Pittsburgh Penguins.

Foreword

THE FIRST TIME I INTERVIEWED SIDNEY CROSBY, I ASKED HIM TO SHARE WITH ME HIS THREE GOALS IN LIFE. HE REPLIED, "PLAY HOCKEY FOR A LIVING, PROVIDE FOR MY FAMILY, AND WIN A STANLEY CUP." ONLY TWENTY YEARS OLD, HE'S ALREADY ACHIEVED TWO OF THOSE THREE GOALS—AND WHO KNOWS, THE THIRD MAY NOT BE FAR OFF. THAT'S SIDNEY CROSBY. UNSELFISH, MATURE BEYOND HIS YEARS, AND BLESSED WITH LASER BEAM FOCUS. TO PUT IT IN SIMPLE TERMS, HE SETS HIS SIGHTS AND ACHIEVES HIS GOALS.

Away from the game of hockey, I don't pretend to know Crosby very well, but what I have seen, I like. Not only is he a proud Nova Scotian, he's even prouder to be a native of Cole Harbour, Nova Scotia. Whether it's during an appearance on *The Tonight Show with Jay Leno*, before the microphones minutes after being selected number one overall at the NHL entry draft, or during a post-game press conference following his Pittsburgh Penguins' debut, geography always comes before celebrity. Where he's from trumps who he is. He's a modest person who comes from humble roots—someone who prefers talking about his family and the people in his neighbourhood to talking about himself. Instead of looking ahead to a career with the Pittsburgh Penguins, he has always insisted on reflecting upon his days in minor hockey, acknowledging the former coaches and teammates who, he says, are a big part of his development. I have always believed these char-

acteristics are paramount to what makes him the central figure in a special story to cover, and in many ways they are the primary reasons he is so revered in his home province.

We don't know if Crosby will break any of Wayne Gretzky's career or single-season scoring records. What we do know is that Sidney Crosby is a young man who brings passion and high purpose to our national game. He has wonderful parents, god-given hockey talent and an outstanding work ethic—all key ingredients that should help lift this young man to the higher echelons of professional hockey.

In arenas across Nova Scotia, like folklore, there are stories about a kid from Cole Harbour who once scored six, seven, even eights points in a game while competing against players three and four years his senior. In junior rinks in Quebec and the Maritimes, fans still whisper about the remarkable teenager who twice led the league in scoring while being named the QMJHL's most valuable player in back-to-back seasons. And now, hockey fans everywhere in the province take what appears to be civic pride when speculating about what Crosby's career stats will look like.

In the end, how do you describe the most exciting hockey player ever to come out of Nova Scotia? How does one find the words to describe a young man blessed with not only an abundance of hockey talent, but also a strong character that is essential to his make-up both on and off the ice? Appropriate prose cannot be applied until the day the curtain comes down on Crosby's NHL career. For now, we can sit back and watch his story evolve, chapter by chapter.

—Paul Hollingsworth

Paul Hollingsworth is an anchor/reporter for CTV (Halifax) and a national correspondent for TSN.

Introduction

As the National Hockey League (NHL) regular season got underway in the fall of 2005, Canadians were hot with hockey fever. Canada was set to defend Olympic titles in Turin, Italy, in 2006, secure in the knowledge that the program of excellence it launched at the beginning of the millennium had made Canada the pre-eminent hockey-playing nation in the world. At every level of Canadian hockey, whether minor, junior, or adult competitive, registrations were growing, and associations were developing a coordinated vision for the sport from coast to coast. The future of hockey never looked brighter.

But it was not the same old game. Hockey was undergoing a profound transition. With the demise of the 2004–2005 NHL season, the glorious generation of Wayne Gretzky and Mario Lemieux came to an abrupt end; with it came the end of a professional hockey era. A labour lockout long in coming forced the NHL and its players to confront issues that had been hurting the league and the sport. Although the short-term pain (a lost 2004–2005 season) was severe, the NHL and the sport of hockey survived, and the outlook for both was very good in 2005.

Convinced that it needed an overhaul to address the lack of creativity and scoring in the game, the NHL enacted a number of rule and style changes that soon began to filter down through the divisions. But the transformation that occurred in the NHL was not just about rules and regulations. There was a definite and marked changing of the guard, and an optimistic feeling about the state of the game. A large part of the optimism had to do with the arrival of a talented young player by the name of Sidney Crosby—the new face of the NHL.

The Rimouski Oceanic graduate and number one draft choice of the Pittsburgh Penguins was a superstar in the making. His stellar hockey career set him up as a future hockey great, to be mentioned alongside Gordie Howe, Gretzky, and Lemieux. Sidney Crosby had the "it" factor—that rare combination of intelligence, talent, and grit that set him above the rest.

Just eighteen years old when he entered the NHL, Sidney Crosby had a tremendous arsenal of weapons at his disposal. There has not been a number one draft choice in recent history who could do it all like number 87 could at such a young age. Before he had even played one NHL game, he could skate, shoot, pass, hit, and lead as well as any of our favourite players. Combine these traits with the fact that he was such a riveting figure—well spoken yet modest—and the National Hockey League had in its midst a player who can lead the charge as the NHL attempts to rival the National Basketball Association (NBA), the National Football League (NFL), and Major League Baseball (MLB) for sports fans' devotion.

For those who have followed this talented forward's career from his days as a terror in the Metro Halifax Minor Hockey Association to more recent times as NHL MVP, it must seem that Sidney Crosby has been destined for greatness since the moment he laced up a pair of skates.

Nowhere were fans more tuned in to Crosby's entrance into the NHL than in Atlantic Canada. Fans from this region cheered heartily for one of their own, someone who played a brand of hockey for which Atlantic Canadians have become notorious. Teams from the Prairies and central Canada will tell you that hockey players from the East Coast are a tough, honest, hard-working lot who neither give nor take a quarter. Although it is true that number 87 has been blessed with the talent to rival any other young hockey player in the world, his grittiness, work ethic, and common touch are what make him a true star in the eyes of Atlantic Canadian hockey fans.

Having recently been named captain of a much-improved and talented team, the former Dartmouth AAA midget star figures to be a fixture in the NHL for a very long time.

East Coast Roots

Atlantic Canada is the birthplace of hockey. With all due respect to the wonderful folks of Kingston, Ontario, and Montreal, Quebec, the splendid sport has its roots in the province of Nova Scotia.

In addition to Thomas C. Haliburton's now-famous account of the noisy boys of Kings College in Windsor, Nova Scotia, playing "hurley on the long pond on the ice" in the early 1800s, periodicals and books from that era also describe "skaters" brandishing "hurleys" (sticks) and suffering the same sorts of aches and ailments that today's hockey players incur. Missing teeth,

Lights, camera, action. Sidney Crosby is a veteran of media relations, having given his first newspaper interview at the age of seven.

FACING PAGE: The rules and the equipment may have changed over the century, but this Dartmouth Hockey League schedule shows that the passion and love for the game remain as strong as ever.

Dartmouth Hockey League

Schedule, 1905.

broken bones, and injuries to the shins are documented in the news journals of the day. Certainly sounds like the game of hockey, doesn't it?

Of course, every city, town, and hamlet in every province and territory in Canada would love to be able to claim the coolest game on earth as its own, but no one will ever convince Atlantic Canadians that the sport now played in every corner of the world does not have its humble beginnings here. If the depth and degree of passion Atlantic Canadians hold for the game is any indicator, hockey could not have begun anywhere else.

For more than one hundred years, hockey players from the East Coast have been successful in forging noteworthy careers in our national sport. Through the decades, these men and women have taken their talent to the national and international stage—and have left an indelible mark on the game of hockey. From the great Gordie Drillon to the amazing Al MacInnis, from the

terrific Thérèse Brisson to the sensational Stacy Wilson, all have done us proud.

Championship hockey teams from the east vying for the right to call themselves Stanley Cup champions were almost commonplace in the early days of Cup competition. Before the National Hockey League claimed Lord Stanley's mug as its own back in 1926, eastern teams regularly held their own championship series play against teams from western and central Canada. Beginning in 1900 and running through the 1912–1913 campaign, no fewer than four Maritime-based hockey clubs battled entries from central Canada for the Stanley Cup.

In the early days of competition, Montreal was home to the best hockey clubs in the land. Following a string of Stanley Cup wins by the Montreal Victorias, the Montreal Shamrocks took over as the city's number one squad. In the 1899–1900 season, on a quest for its second straight cup, the Shamrocks played host to Atlantic Canada's first Stanley Cup challenger, the Halifax Crescents.

Led by a very stingy defence, the Crescents were hoping they could avoid a shootout with the heavily favoured Montreal club. It was a game plan that up to that time had put them in good stead. With a forward unit that tended to overwhelm opponents with fast skating and aggressive checking, Halifax had streamrolled oppo-

Gordie Drillon

Gordie Drillon of Moncton, New Brunswick, was a decorated veteran of the National Hockey League when he retired. A Lady Byng Trophy winner in 1938, Drillon also led the league in scoring that season with 52 points. The consummate team player, the Maple Leaf legend was an all-star in 1938 and 1939 and a Stanley Cup winner in 1942. Although he'll always be remembered as a Toronto Maple Leaf, the Hockey Hall of Fame inductee ended his NHL career as a Hab in 1943.

Al MacInnis

Al MacInnis of Inverness, Nova Scotia, retired in 2005 having played nearly 1,500 games in the National Hockey League. A Norris Trophy winner for best defenceman in 1998–1999, MacInnis also won the Conn Smythe Trophy in 1989 with the Stanley Cup–winning Calgary Flames. A member of the Team Canada squad that captured Olympic gold in Salt Lake City in 2002, the hard-shooting rearguard scored an impressive 1,274 points as a member of the Flames and the St. Louis Blues.

Thérèse Brisson

To many, Thérèse Brisson is the first superstar of women's hockey. The former University of New Brunswick professor played on six world championship squads and was an integral member of Team Canada's gold medal club at the 2002 Olympics. A rock-solid defender who enjoyed the physical part of the game, Brisson joined Team Canada in the mid-1990s and was captain for three years following the 1998 Olympics.

Stacy Wilson

Stacy Wilson of Moncton, New Brunswick, was the very first national women's Olympic hockey team captain. Wilson, a veteran of many national and world championships, led Canada to a silver medal in Nagano, Japan, in 1998. A fiery competitor famous for her work ethic on and off the ice, Wilson moved into the coaching ranks following her retirement, and even had time to write a hockey book for girls in 2000.

These distinguished athletes are the members of the 1898 Halifax Crescents. The capital city club, seen here with the Starr Manufacturing Trophy, was that year's Halifax Hockey League champions.

nents throughout the regular and post-season. The Shamrocks, however, were a machine the likes of which Halifax had never encountered.

Despite a valiant effort, the Montreal Shamrocks were just too much for Halifax. The Crescents could not contain the vaunted Montreal offence, and Halifax returned to Nova Scotia victims of 10–2 and 11–0 beatings. The Crescents were no doubt disappointed with the result, but their groundbreaking efforts laid the foundation for other regional clubs confident they could break central Canada's hold on the title.

Buoyed by Halifax's appearance in the Stanley Cup series, two more Nova Scotia–based entries and a New Brunswick side, hungry to bring Atlantic Canada its first Cup victory, also found themselves only one series win away from raising Lord Stanley's Cup aloft.

In 1906, the New Glasgow Cubs, bent on enacting a measure of revenge, tangled with the fabled Montreal Wanderers. Hoping to accomplish what the Halifax Crescents could not, the Cubs headed west. As with the Crescents, though, New Glasgow would meet a Montreal team with just too many weapons. Unable to handle the Wanderers' ferocious attack in game one, New Glasgow fought back

gamely and played extremely well in game two. The affair was close throughout, with Montreal eventually pulling out a 7–2 decision on home ice. Finding solace in their second-place finish, the pride of Pictou County returned home with a historic playoff run behind them.

In 1912 and 1913, the Moncton Victorias and the Sydney Miners were the first back-to-back Atlantic Canadian challengers in Stanley Cup history. Both Moncton and Sydney suffered two-game sweeps at the hands of the Quebec Bulldogs, but the defeats were as much about bad timing as bad performances. In most years, either one of these terrific hockey clubs could have won the Stanley Cup outright. Unfortunately, this was the era of the magnificent Joe Malone and the dynamic Quebec Bulldogs, and no team, at that time, was their equal.

In addition to Hall of Famer Joe Malone, Quebec's lineup in 1912–1913 included the stingy Paddy Moran in net as well as famed wingers Tommy Smith and Rusty Crawford. At the height of his career, Malone was a one-man wrecking crew, scoring nine times against Sydney to become one of only a handful of players to score more than eight goals in a Stanley Cup game.

The Bulldogs' reign would last only long enough to deny the Victorias and Miners. Unbelievably, considering how powerful they were, the Quebec Bulldogs would not successfully challenge for another Cup, yet in consecutive years the short-lived dynasty forced two excellent Maritime entries to settle for second place. The Sydney challenge in 1913 would be the last for a team from the east.

In 1926, the National Hockey League took over sole ownership of the trophy, and the dreams of bringing Lord Stanley's mug back to the birthplace of hockey had to be abandoned.

While Atlantic Canadian hockey clubs may have ceased being able to compete for the Stanley Cup after 1926, a steady stream of hockey players continued to play significant and starring roles in professional hockey. On the heels of extraordinary players such as Willie O'Ree, a sort of "golden age" for Atlantic Canada–born hockey players in professional hockey began. From 1965 onward, a plethora of regional elite athletes would rise to the highest ranks of pro hockey: Danny Grant, Keith Brown, Al MacAdam, Gerard Gallant, Gordie Gallant, Bobby Smith, Wendell Young—on and on goes the list of Atlantic Canadians who enjoyed stellar careers in either the National Hockey League or the World Hockey Association.

Success at the professional and international levels has always been the big prize for Atlantic Canadian hockey players, but it would be wrong to think that Atlantic Canada's hockey heritage is all about the professional ranks. The region has also enjoyed incredible success at the amateur and collegiate level.

The Canadian Interuniversity Sport (CIS) championships, emblematic of university hockey superiority, have become a source of pride for a couple of Atlantic schools: The University of Moncton and Acadia University have become collegiate powers in men's hockey, winning six national titles between them.

The Allan Cup, arguably the toughest prize to win in Canadian amateur hockey, has landed in each of the four Atlantic Provinces in the past two decades. Corner Brook, Charlottetown, Saint John, and Truro have each taken turns bringing the senior AAA championship home.

There has also been success in women's hockey. Refusing to be intimidated by much bigger associations coming out of Quebec and Ontario, regional and provincial clubs from the East Coast are taking on the very best competition in the nation and have been distinguishing themselves on a regular basis. One need only look at the results of the Esso Women's Nationals and the fact that Atlantic Canadians continue to contribute big numbers to the national women's program to see how successful women's hockey is in the region.

Hockey for the Future

The successes of the past few decades have helped breed an aura of confidence among young athletes in Atlantic Canada as they strive to reach their dreams of someday playing professional or international hockey. Sidney Crosby is no doubt a product of the great developmental program that has taken root, and his success will in turn spur young hockey players to pursue their athletic goals.

Indeed, Sidney Crosby has become a terrific source of inspiration for hockey players across the region. As noteworthy as his hockey heroics have been, Crosby's class and grace off the ice have

Willie O'Ree

New Brunswick–born hockey player Willie O'Ree forever changed the face of the National Hockey League. The Fredericton native broke the colour barrier in the NHL when the Boston Bruins, unable to deny O'Ree's abundant skills any longer, called him up in January of 1958. O'Ree enjoyed a remarkable career, retiring with the San Diego Hawks of the Pacific Hockey League in 1979. O'Ree helped pave the way for players as the director of youth development for the NHL diversity program.

> *YOU CAN'T PRACTISE WHAT CROSBY HAS. IT'S JUST NATURAL. WHEN SIDNEY CROSBY IS ON THE ICE, YOU CATCH YOURSELF CONTINUALLY WATCHING NUMBER 87 BECAUSE YOU KNOW AT SOME POINT THE PUCK WILL RETURN TO HIM AND THAT HE WILL DO SOMETHING SPECIAL WITH IT. OFF THE ICE YOU'RE SO IMPRESSED BY THE WAY HE HANDLES HIMSELF ... AND MORE IMPORTANTLY HOW HE HANDLES OTHERS.*
> — Mario Durocher, former coach of Canada's national junior team

FACING PAGE: The summer of 2002 saw Sidney Crosby make one of the most important decisions of his life. The Dartmouth Subways grad is seen sifting through the mound of recruitment packages sent to him. Eventually the fourteen-year-old phenom would settle on Shattuck–St. Mary's prep school in Faribault, Minnesota.

been just as impressive, maybe more so. In an era when too many promising young athletes are seen rushing into the stands to confront fans or berating teammates and opponents alike, Sidney Crosby has been a terrific role model for the thousands of Canadian boys and girls who watch him and realize that they too can reach the highest levels of our favourite national sport.

With young stars such as New Glasgow's Colin White, a two-time Stanley Cup winner with New Jersey; P.E.I.'s Brad Richards, who won the Lady Byng Trophy, the Conn Smythe Trophy, and the Stanley Cup in 2004 with Tampa Bay; and Newfoundland's Michael Ryder, an up-and-comer in Montreal, also thriving in the National Hockey League, it certainly appears that Atlantic Canada is about to place itself at the forefront of the professional hockey scene. The region's governing bodies have made an unprecedented commitment to the sport, and it is beginning to pay huge dividends.

Every region of Canada has now sent a young man to the professional ranks to act as its ambassador. In the 1940s and 1950s, a young man from Floral, Saskatchewan, became hockey's first superstar. "Mr. Hockey," as Gordie Howe is known, helped carry the NHL on his shoul-

ders until two young men from Ontario arrived to lighten the load. In the 1970s and 1980s respectively, an extraordinary defenceman from Parry Sound and a scoring sensation from Brantford brought the sport of hockey to prime time. Bobby Orr and Wayne Gretzky combined talents and charisma, helping to raise hockey's profile to the level of football, baseball, and basketball on the North American sports scene.

The last decade saw Quebec's magnificent Mario Lemieux play the game of hockey with a magic that brought patrons of NHL arenas to their feet. Now, it's Atlantic Canada's turn. Nova Scotia's Sidney Crosby is a power forward with unmatchable speed and soft hands. It is a triple threat that no player—with the possible exception of Lemieux—has possessed.

All things being equal, if fate is kind to Sidney Crosby and allows him to play out his career without falling prey to serious injury or other unfortunate circumstance, the young man from Cole Harbour should have a special NHL career indeed.

THE ODYSSEY BEGINS

COLE HARBOUR, NOVA SCOTIA, IS A CHARMING, CLOSE-KNIT COMMUNITY LOCATED IN THE HALIFAX REGIONAL MUNICIPALITY. IN THIS SUBURBAN, MIDDLE-CLASS PART OF DARTMOUTH, LIFE REVOLVES AROUND SCHOOL, WORK, AND SPORTS, WITH THE POPULAR COLE HARBOUR PLACE AT THE CENTRE. THE COMMUNITY FACILITY, WHICH INCLUDES TWO RINKS, A LIBRARY, A SWIMMING POOL, AND TENNIS AND SQUASH COURTS, THRUMS WITH LIFE. WITH A COMBINED DARTMOUTH–COLE HARBOUR POPULATION OF JUST OVER EIGHTY THOUSAND, THE REGION IS A BUSY URBAN CENTRE WITH A RURAL PASTORAL FEEL.

While the fixed white cap of the Cole Harbour Lighthouse that looks out over Tor Bay sheds light on a past where mariners ruled the era of wind and water, the local Heritage Farm Museum pays homage to the role that agriculture played in the hamlet founded in the early 1700s. Cole Harbour is most famous for the role it played in the American Revolutionary War of the mid-1700s, acting as a place of refuge for the thousands of Loyalists who left Boston and New York. That claim to fame is about to be overshadowed by an unlikely modern-day hero—a teenage hockey phenom poised to change the landscape of professional hockey.

On August 7, 1987, Sidney Crosby was born in Halifax to Troy and Trina Crosby. Troy Crosby, a native of Halifax himself,

had recently returned home following a major junior hockey career in Verdun that saw him taken in the twelfth round of the 1984 draft by the Montreal Canadiens. It would not take long before his son exhibited a passion for the game as well.

Still a little too young to be streaking down the ice at the local arena, a two-and-a-half-year-old Sidney Crosby retreated to the family basement for his formal introduction to the game of hockey. Using red, white, and blue paint to mimic the contours of a hockey arena, Troy Crosby built his son a hockey hideaway that would allow him the opportunity to hone his skills until it was time to strap on the skates and take his game to the backyard rink.

Quick FACTS

In a sign of things to come, fourteen-year-old Sidney Crosby was featured on the CBC television special *Hockey Day in Canada*.

Sidney Crosby's numbers at Shattuck–St. Mary's were nothing less than spectacular. In a mere fifty-seven games, the first-year phenom scored a remarkable 72 goals and 90 assists for 162 points.

FACING PAGE: Troy, Trina, and Sidney Crosby in June of 2003, soon after hearing that the Shattuck–St. Mary's graduate had been drafted first overall by the Rimouski Oceanic of the QMJHL.

According to Sidney Crosby's own accounts, he was bent on spending every available free moment practising his favourite sport. Long after he had learned to skate, Sidney continued to retreat to the "Crosby Coliseum" to nurture his incredible shooting skills. The countless hours devoted to everything hockey would pay off when the time came for him to join the metro minor hockey scene.

From the moment Sidney Crosby first hit the ice at the tender age of three, it was obvious that the lad could not get enough of the game of hockey. It was also pretty clear that he had been blessed with some incredible talent. Barely old enough to start school, Sidney became something of a local hockey star. Possessing the skills of a player twice his age, the boy was ripping up the metro minor hockey leagues and leaving awe-inspired opponents, teammates, and fans shaking their heads at what they were witnessing.

Regardless of the division, Sidney Crosby was racking up 100-plus-point seasons with regularity and making believers out of teammates and opponents alike. Gary Knickle became a convert when he watched a ten-year-old Sidney tearing up pee wee hockey against his nephew's team: "He's always played with kids three or four years older than him," says Knickle. "It's not so much his hockey, it's his personality and how he carries himself. He shows his maturity" (Canadian Press). At ten years old, Sidney Crosby's hockey profile and stature were growing.

Any time a young hockey phenom starts to put up astronomical numbers and begins to fill arenas the way Sidney Crosby did back in the 1990s, it is only a matter of time before the Canadian media begin to take an interest. In Sidney Crosby's case, he gave his first newspaper interview at the ripe age of seven, although he had been on the radar of national media sources before that. "It was incredible to see the interest in this child athlete," comments Peter Assaff, reporter for the *Northern Light* (Bathurst). "Right away you could see that there was something more to this kid than just goals and assists and the ability to play hockey. Sidney Crosby already had this star quality about him, and Canadians wanted to know as much about him as they could."

By the 2001–2002 hockey season, Sidney Crosby had become a household name—in hockey circles, anyway—from coast to coast. As a fourteen-year-old forward with the Dartmouth Subways, he was about to embark on the most important season of his life. For young hockey players like Crosby who are seriously eyeing the NHL, midget hockey is known as the make-it-or-break-it division. To play professional hockey, players need to make their mark at this level, where the pool is bigger and opponents stronger and faster.

While there was never any debate about his skills, nor his ability to put up big numbers, as Sidney Crosby prepared to play his final season in Dartmouth, there were still some observers who questioned whether the fourteen-year-old could match the enormous expectations laid out for him. A national midget tournament in "the City by the Bay" would provide the answers.

2

UNBEATABLE IN BATHURST: THE 2002 AIR CANADA CUP

ALTHOUGH SIDNEY CROSBY PUT FORTH MANY OUTSTANDING MINOR HOCKEY PERFORMANCES, IT WAS A
SINGULAR TOURNAMENT, AND IN PARTICULAR ONE AWE-INSPIRING GAME AGAINST THE RED DEER CHIEFS, THAT
SET IN MOTION THE EVENTS THAT WOULD LEAD HIM TO BECOME THIS GENERATION'S HOCKEY ICON. SIDNEY
CROSBY USED THE 2002 AIR CANADA CUP, HOSTED BY THE CITY OF BATHURST, NEW BRUNSWICK, TO EXPLODE
ONTO THE NORTH AMERICAN HOCKEY SCENE. THE TOURNAMENT MARKED THE BEGINNING OF A JOURNEY THAT
WOULD SEE HIM BECOME THE EVENTUAL NUMBER ONE PICK IN THE 2005 NHL ENTRY DRAFT, AND PLACE AN
EXCLAMATION MARK ON THE END OF A SPECTACULAR MINOR HOCKEY CAREER IN CANADA.

2002 may well be remembered as the year Sidney Crosby ceased being a local prodigious child talent who amazed patrons of his hometown arena with his athleticism and ability and instead became a bona fide national treasure who was being groomed as professional hockey's heir apparent. The year was noteworthy for Crosby for a number of reasons. There were the numerous on-ice accomplishments and sports milestones he attained one after another, but there were also intriguing off-ice matters that appeared in 2002, specifically a heart-wrenching, life-altering hockey

decision that Crosby and his family would need to make. It is a choice that many other talented young athletes before him have had to make, a virtual rite of passage.

A fifteen-month whirlwind stretch from April 2002 to June 2003 witnessed the transformation of the Cole Harbour, Nova Scotia, minor hockey player from a local to a national to an international hockey name. With amazing speed, Sidney Crosby's hockey and personal life took on new form, and it all began in a northern New Brunswick city that would ultimately share

> **THE CITY WAS ALREADY VERY EXCITED ABOUT HOSTING THE NATIONAL CHAMPIONSHIPS. BUT WHEN WORD GOT AROUND THAT SIDNEY CROSBY WAS COMING TO TOWN TO PLAY, THE EXCITEMENT AND ANTICIPATION ROSE TO ANOTHER LEVEL.**
>
> —Peter Assaff, *Northern Light* (Bathurst)

more than one of the young man's defining moments.

In April of 2002, the city of Bathurst was electric in anticipation of playing host to a national hockey championship. The 2002 Air Canada Cup midget championships were to be decided in "the City by the Bay," and the hockey-mad fans of Chaleur were ecstatic.

Since its successful attempt at landing a Quebec Major Junior Hockey League (QMJHL) franchise in 1998 (Acadie-Bathurst Titan), the city had put forth concerted efforts to attract high-profile hockey events for its brand-spanking-new K. C. Irving Regional Centre. Since few national hockey tournaments are bigger or have a higher profile than the storied national midget finals, it seemed that the whole of northern New Brunswick had become enthralled with the bid. The event took on even greater proportions when it became official that the Dartmouth Subway AAA squad and their teenage phenom Sidney Crosby would be in attendance as Team Atlantic's representative.

For some hockey purists, Sidney Crosby's play in this tournament would determine if all the hype surrounding him had been warranted. For years,

Sidney Crosby's acumen in the faceoff circle was developed very early in his career. The Dartmouth Subway centreman is seen taking another crucial draw at the 2002 Air Canada Cup in Bathurst, NB.

word had been spreading about this young hockey sensation—years ahead of his peers, a once-in-a-lifetime talent who could do amazing things on the ice. This tournament without a doubt would be Sidney Crosby's stiffest challenge to date, and because it was being held on a national stage, its significance would be magnified. Of course, this would not be the first time Sidney Crosby was tested against rival national competition, but undeniably it would be one of the most important.

Sidney Crosby needed to go to Bathurst and perform well, put up some impressive numbers, and show that he could play through being the marked man. Every team playing against Dartmouth was going to key on Crosby, and he needed to show that he could produce despite the constant attention he'd receive from opposing checkers. Indeed, Crosby would be expected to stand out among the midget-aged elite, most of whom were feeling the pressure of trying to impress major junior or college scouts themselves.

One of the questions that dogged Sidney Crosby was going to be addressed in Bathurst as well. Could he still be dominant against players who were taller and bigger? Like the elephant in the room that could no longer be ignored, the question of size and physical strength that had some people unsure of Crosby's future needed to be addressed.

Professional hockey has long been a big man's game. Marcel Dionne and Theoren Fleury aside, dreams of playing pro hockey have become the domain of those six feet tall or taller and two-hundred-plus pounds. Although Sidney Crosby is not a small man by most standards, his physical stature had been a focal point of critics. Convinced his frame could not stand up to the increased punishment it would need to endure the closer he got to the pro ranks, doubters knew the national midget tournament would force-feed Crosby a steady diet of big, fast, talented combatants bent on wearing him down and taking him out of the game. If they succeeded in minimizing the star forward and his impact on games, the critics' concerns would prove justified.

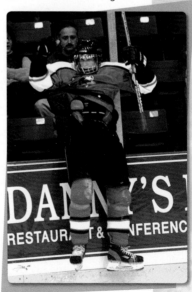

Sidney Crosby celebrates another Team Atlantic score. The fourteen-year-old did a lot of celebrating at the national midget championship, taking home both the top scorer and most valuable player awards at the event.

ABOVE: Though few observers gave Team Atlantic much of a chance at winning gold at the 2002 Air Canada Cup, Sidney Crosby and his mates nearly pulled it off, going the distance before losing 6–2 to Tisdale, Saskatchewan, in the final.

the Canadian Hockey League (CHL) ranks, or it would see him fail and take a significant step backwards in what to that point had been a meteoric and unblemished rise.

Hockey fans in Bathurst had waited a long time for this calibre of hockey to come to their city. The patience the fans and organizers had shown was rewarded with some truly spectacular play. Unlike in years past, the national midget-aged talent pool was extremely deep in 2002, and each and every regional rep at this event belonged. Parity at long last appeared to have arrived in Canadian amateur hockey, and the state of the game was healthier than ever.

In the days leading up to the official opening, fans were salivating at the prospect of seeing Sidney Crosby lead Team Atlantic against the best midget-aged talent in the nation; one game in particular, though, stands head and shoulders above them all. On Wednesday, April 24, the Pacific representatives, the Red Deer Chiefs, would take on Team Atlantic rep Dartmouth, and followers of the event knew that this match had all the earmarks of a classic.

The Red Deer Chiefs played a typical western Canadian style of hockey. The Chiefs were big, rugged, and fast, and they finished their checks with a ferocity that intimidated most opponents. In their key round-robin match against Team Atlantic, their game plan was obvious to all: Place a bull's eye on Sidney Crosby's jersey, and hit him at every opportunity. Every time Crosby touched the puck, and maybe a few times when he didn't, he was to be punished.

Northern New Brunswick played a big role in Sidney Crosby's hockey life in 2002 and 2003. After leading his Dartmouth AAA Subways to the Air Canada Cup in Bathurst in April of 2002, Crosby returned to the region the following winter as a member of Team Nova Scotia during the Canada Winter Games held in Campbellton-Bathurst.

Facing Page: Sidney Crosby's final season as a member of the Darmouth AAA Subways saw him put up some spectacular numbers, including a franchise record 106 goals scored in 81 games.

As unfair as it may seem, on the eve of the championships, Sidney Crosby's young career was already at a crossroads. This was a week that was either going to see him take his game to another level and set the stage for his eventual leap to

Even for a guy as tough as Sidney Crosby, who is not known for shying away from the rough stuff, the task of playing through the chaos and getting on the scoreboard must have seemed a daunting one. "Everyone in the building, including probably Sidney Crosby, knew what Red Deer's game plan was going to be," notes Crosby's Dartmouth Subways coach Brad Crossley. "Nail Crosby at every turn, and make him a non-issue in the game."

The game plan may have been sound, but someone obviously forgot to tell Sidney Crosby. He was unstoppable, despite the Chiefs' best efforts to hit him at every turn. Against the feared Red Deer machine from Alberta, Crosby scored a natural hat trick and added two assists as the Subways surged to a 5–0 first period lead.

The western reps must have wondered what had hit them as shift after shift Crosby disposed of opposing checkers and double teams to find the back of the net. Crosby would not be denied. It was an awesome sight to watch him defy Red Deer to use physical force to stop him and then dispose of the tight checking on his way to potting another goal. It was a period of hockey for the ages and one still talked about by those in attendance. "Sidney Crosby was determined to send a message not only to the Red Deer Chiefs, but to anyone who doubted his ability to be a star on the national stage," adds coach Crossley.

Ultimately, Dartmouth's substantial first period lead evaporated as Red Deer's vaunted offensive arsenal kicked in. The Alberta squad eventually found their game, and the underdog Dartmouth Subways were subdued 8–6. The final outcome that afternoon quickly became an afterthought, an irrelevant asterisk linked to one of the truly superior solo efforts in event lore. Sidney Crosby had proved that when confronted with the best midget-aged hockey opposition in the nation, he was still head and shoulders above them. He was the best of the best in his age group, and the gap between him and everyone else seemed to be growing.

Of course, the round-robin match would not be the last the Red Deer Chiefs would see of

Quick FACTS

In November of 2003, Sidney Crosby made headlines across North America with the infamous "lacrosse goal" he scored against the Quebec Remparts.

While with the Rimouski Oceanic, Sidney Crosby became the first player to win the prestigious CHL Player of the Year award in consecutive seasons (2003–2004, 2004–2005).

Sidney Crosby won the Guy Lafleur Trophy (most valuable player in the QMJHL playoffs) on the strength of a spectacular post-season total of 31 points in 13 games.

Quick FACTS

In a round-robin match at the 2002 Air Canada Cup in Bathurst, New Brunswick, Sidney Crosby scored five unanswered points in the first period against the powerhouse Red Deer Chiefs. Crosby's three-goal, two-assist opening-frame effort vaulted him onto the national hockey stage.

ABOVE: Sidney Crosby prepares to take to the ice at the K. C. Irving Regional Centre. The city of Bathurst was electric with the news that Sidney Crosby would be coming to town to participate in the 2002 Air Canada Cup.

FACING PAGE: Sidney Crosby enjoying a brief respite from the rink. J. P. Parisé, Shattuck–St. Mary's director of hockey operations, marvelled at the way the young superstar handled all of the attention with quiet grace and a maturity well beyond his years.

Sidney Crosby. Determined to savour the sweet taste of revenge, Crosby and his mates would turn the tables on the Chiefs on semifinal Saturday. Displaying a flare for dramatics that had become as much a part of his game as goals and assists, Sidney Crosby scored a power play marker with thirty-two seconds remaining in the game to give his team a 4–3 come-from-behind victory. The last-minute heroics propelled Dartmouth into the finals and sent rival Red Deer to the proverbial showers.

To Crosby's most ardent fans and harshest critics, the tournament proved to be a revelation. To those not previously sold on his game, Crosby emphatically answered all remaining questions. And to those who believed in the young man's talent, even they must have been surprised at just how good he was. In the end, his sensational play in Bathurst underscored something more than the obvious fact that Sidney Crosby was indeed the best minor hockey player in Canada. Having faced

down every hurdle that had come his way during his years in Nova Scotia, it was clear that Sidney Crosby faced the biggest decision in his life—whether or not to leave home to pursue his hockey dreams.

AIR CANADA CUP TOURNAMENT STATISTICS, BATHURST, N.B., APRIL 2002

	GP	G	A	P	PIM	GWG
Sidney Crosby	5	8	10	18	6	2

YOUNG MAN GOES WEST

SIDNEY CROSBY'S DOMINATING PERFORMANCE AT THE 2002 AIR CANADA CUP IN BATHURST UNDERLINED THE NEED FOR THE TALENTED YOUNG MAN TO SEEK OUT NEW CHALLENGES. HAVING ACCOMPLISHED EVERYTHING HE COULD IN ATLANTIC CANADA, HE WAS FACED WITH THE PROSPECT OF LEAVING HOME TO PURSUE HIS HOCKEY GOALS.

The spring of 2002 saw Sidney Crosby quickly approaching a crossroads … and the path he chose would decide his future in the game. For most small-town Canadians who dream of playing in the NHL, there comes a moment when they must face the heart-wrenching reality that advancing their careers will mean leaving home. It had probably been a moment that Sidney Crosby knew would arrive; still, for a boy of fourteen, one can only imagine how agonizing it was to think of leaving home so young.

In his autobiography, *The Great One*, Wayne Gretzky admits that one of the most difficult decisions he had to make in his life was to leave home at the age of fourteen. With few if any hockey challenges remaining in his hometown of

Brantford, Ontario, a teenage Gretzky grudgingly acknowledged the need to leave the safety and security of his boyhood home for the opportunity to play in the famed Toronto minor hockey system.

Certainly Sidney Crosby had some of the same misgivings in the summer of 2002. But the need to leave his Nova Scotia home, as painful as it must have been, would have been clear. The kind of competition that Crosby needed in order to adequately prepare for a role in major junior hockey could only be found elsewhere. In time, the question evolved from whether or not to leave to where his new hockey home would be. For the potential number one pick in the 2003 junior entry draft, it was a decision not to be taken lightly.

Quick FACTS

In 2002–2003, Sidney Crosby packed up his hockey bag and headed west, where he attended Shattuck–St. Mary's prep school in Faribault, Minnesota, helping the Sabres to a U.S. national midget championship.

In 1967, the National Hockey League held a monumental expansion. Six new hockey clubs—the St. Louis Blues, Minnesota North Stars, Philadelphia Flyers, Los Angeles Kings, California Seals, and Pittsburgh Penguins—joined the "original six" clubs in the new-look NHL.

In many respects, Sidney Crosby's 2002–2003 season would act as a bridge. He needed to get from where he was, a minor hockey superstar with unlimited potential, to where he was going, the number one, most sought after junior hockey player in the Canadian Hockey League.

Sidney Crosby's camp understood that he needed to be challenged, he needed to be groomed, he needed to be surrounded by hockey people who understood what this year was about. The Cole Harbour native needed to go to an organization that would allow him the opportunity to develop not only as a hockey player but also as a person. It also needed to provide Sidney Crosby the opportunity to attain a national hockey championship.

Any number of teams would have deemed it an out-and-out coup to land a player of Crosby's stature, but eventually the impressive list of potential hockey homes got whittled down to one midwestern prep school. It was a selection that was as intriguing to some as it was surprising.

Shattuck–St. Mary's prep school is located in Faribault, Minnesota. The school had enjoyed a history of success prior to 2002–2003, and Sidney Crosby was brought on board to help the Sabres win another national championship.

Despite its storied hockey history, the small and somewhat unremarkable midwestern institution appeared to some to be an odd choice as the new home for the budding hockey superstar. A closer look and it becomes clear why this prairie powerhouse was actually perfect.

To begin with, the relatively low profile of Shattuck–St. Mary's added to its attractiveness. The onslaught of media and other distractions, at least early on, was not as great here as it would have been had Crosby remained in Canada or attended an East Coast institution. The young man would certainly benefit from the early anonymity while he adjusted to his new surroundings.

In addition, one of the prerequisites in choosing a school was the ability to surround Crosby with established hockey people. At Shattuck–St. Mary's, the hockey program director had direct ties to one of Canada's most glorious hockey moments. In 1972, J. P. Parisé was a member of Team Canada during the unforgettable Summit Series against the USSR. The Minnesota North Stars winger had become infamous for his role in a game-eight uprising against West German referee Kompalla, which ended with Parisé's ejection from the deciding match.

Thirty years later, Parisé had completed the impressive transition from NHL star to prep-school administrator, and he would be seen as the perfect mentor for Sidney Crosby. With Parisé's son Zach, a graduate of the Sabres program, also on the cusp of accelerating his own pro hockey aspirations, it must have seemed like an ideal situation.

More and more it appeared that the decision to go to Faribault was the right one, and after some initial trepidation and concerns about the unfamiliar surroundings both on and off the ice, Sidney Crosby began to show everyone why he was pegged as the best midget-aged hockey prospect in North America.

With fellow standouts Jack Johnson and Drew Stafford riding shotgun, Sidney Crosby helped the Sabres get out of the gate quickly—and they did not look back. In approximately seventy games, Shattuck–St. Mary's sported a win-loss record of well over .500. The club travelled extensively in the United States and Canada and racked up impressive victory after impressive victory, including two over long-time Canadian arch-rivals the Calgary Royals and the Edmonton Canadians.

With Sidney Crosby firing on all cylinders, the Sabres finished the 2002–2003 season playing perhaps their best hockey of the year. As the regular season drew to a close, there was absolutely no doubt that Crosby's outstanding performance had locked up his status as the number one pick at the upcoming QMJHL June draft. With his standing as the number one junior prospect in the world assured, Sidney Crosby took aim at the national championship.

As the playoffs began, the familiar story of opponents centring their entire game plan on shutting down Sidney Crosby came to the fore. The U.S. national midget championship would be settled in the nation's capital, and Sidney Crosby was aware that a number of familiar opponents would descend on the District of Columbia bent on denying him the title.

Sabres bench boss Tom Ward knew his club was in tough, but there was something about Sidney Crosby's demeanour that had a calming influence on both the coach and his club: "You could sense that Sidney felt very confident about his game and also very secure in how well the team had been playing prior to the national championship."

A veteran of these national midget championships himself, coach Ward also noticed a heightened degree of determination and focus by the rookie. "I could sense heading into the playoffs that Sidney was not going to be denied. It was exciting to see how Sidney had

The most impressive weapon in Sidney Crosby's arsenal may be his tremendous shot.

prepared himself for the moment. He was an important cog in a talented and veteran team that as a collective group recognized the importance of another national championship to the Shattuck–St. Mary's hockey program." Ward's keen intuition was dead on: Sidney Crosby would end up playing some of the best hockey of his life in the 2003 post-season.

The Shattuck–St. Mary's Sabres would need to dispose of some familiar foes to once again reign as national champions … and Sidney Crosby would need to be the X factor against some very tough competition. The Eastern Massachusetts Senators were a skilled team that featured as many offensive weapons as the Sabres. All things being equal, the Senators may have been the Sabres' biggest competition and an awesome early threat, but Sidney Crosby would prove to be too much for the team from New England. The Sabres escaped with a victory and the right to move on.

The Little Caesars team from Detroit, Michigan, and the Midget Tier 1 Stars from Dallas, Texas, were the next to confront Sidney Crosby and his Shattuck–St. Mary's side. The Little Caesars squad had played well against the Sabres in the past, earning a reputation for tough, aggressive play. The Dallas Stars, on the other hand, were known for balance and depth and their consistency of play. Knowing full well that all roads to the national championship went through Sidney Crosby, both clubs took aim at the Sabres' leading scorer. If their intent was to intimidate Crosby and put him off his game, their plan backfired in a huge way.

Confronting perhaps the most sustained physical opposition in quite some time, Crosby both dished out and absorbed a lot of punishment. The physical play seemed to inspire him even more as he helped engineer wins over both Detroit and Dallas. There is no doubt that opponents enjoyed some success in slowing down the Shattuck–St. Mary's star, but as the Senators, Little Caesars, and Stars all found out, Sidney Crosby was becoming adept at making the on-ice adjustments needed to deal with the strategies opposing coaches were throwing at him.

The final obstacle to the national championship came in the form of the very skilled and very hungry Team Illinois, whose big guns included five-foot, ten-inch sniper Kyle Acre, as well as the strong goaltending tandem of Johnny Riley and Mike Devoney.

> **SIDNEY CROSBY ALWAYS HANDLED HIMSELF EXTREMELY WELL. WITH ALL OF THE DISTRACTIONS AND DISRUPTION THAT HE HAS HAD TO ENDURE THIS YEAR, FOR HIM TO BE ABLE TO COMPORT HIMSELF THE WAY HE HAS AND TO HAVE THE KIND OF SEASON HE IS HAVING ON THE ICE, I THINK IT SAYS A LOT ABOUT HIS CHARACTER AND HIS DESIRE.**
>
> —J. P. Parisé, director of hockey operations, Shattuck–St. Mary's

Sidney Crosby and the other Sabres forwards would face their stiffest challenge to date. Illinois boasted a solid defensive corps and an opportunistic forward attack that specialized in capitalizing on goal-scoring chances. The midwestern hockey team was also a confident bunch, having posted a gold medal victory earlier in the season at the prestigious Mac Midget Hockey Tournament in Calgary, Alberta.

As expected, the final was an out-and-out war. Like a Frazier–Ali fight, both teams threw their best punches without garnering a knock-down. With ten minutes left in the game, Shattuck–St. Mary's was up by two and thwarting every offensive thrust put forth by the Illinois club. As time became a factor, it looked as though Team Illinois had run out of answers for the stifling Sabres trap, as had been the case throughout the 2002–2003 season.

However, the Illinois players were also at their most dangerous when their backs were up against the wall. With less than a minute left in the game, Team Illinois pulled their goaltender. After a frantic scramble in front of the Sabres net, J. J. Evans tucked the puck behind the surprised Shattuck–St. Mary's keeper, and Team Illinois had pulled within one. Team Illinois had recaptured the momentum and looked as if they were primed to tie the affair, but the boys from Minnesota had not come this far to be denied the gold, and the Sabres would hang on for the 5–4 victory.

The national championship capped a sensational season for Sidney Crosby. In fifty-seven games played, he accumulated 72 goals and 90 assists for 162 points. The points-per-game average of almost 3 was absolutely off the chart—and it still did not do justice to the strength of his play, game in and game out.

Perhaps the most important accomplishment in 2002–2003 for Sidney Crosby was the title victory. He had proved that he could take a team on his shoulders and make it a winner. The centreman had succeeded in making every Sabres player around him better, a talent shared by all great ones. With all his pre-season aspirations seemingly met, Sidney Crosby would be able to return to Canada from his one-

Quick FACTS

Sidney Crosby was all of sixteen years, four months, and twenty-four days old when he established a World Junior Championship record by becoming the youngest player to score a goal. Crosby achieved the historic feat on December 28, 2003, during a 7–2 Team Canada win over Switzerland.

year hiatus and take a well-deserved break from the frenetic pace.

While Shattuck–St. Mary's may have provided Sidney Crosby some early respite, as his accomplishments and profile began to skyrocket, so did the demands of fans, the media, and a public hungry to know more about him. It must have been difficult trying to juggle all of these requests while still trying to devote his energies to making his hockey club a winner.

Through it all, though, Crosby remained approachable, humble, and personable. The Shattuck–St. Mary's experience was not just about the growth of his game; it was also about his evolution as a person. As happy as those close to him were with his on-ice advancement, Sidney Crosby's obvious development as a confident, mature, articulate young man must have made friends and family proud. Even more impressive was that he was able to foster this evolution as the demands on his time and his energies increased markedly.

You can be certain that the Rimouski Oceanic of the QMJHL had also been taking stock of Crosby's ability both to stay cool and to lead a franchise to the winner's circle. With only months left before the 2003 QMJHL entry draft, Rimouski ownership must have felt as if they were holding the winning lottery ticket.

Even on vacation Sidney Crosby was never very far from the game of hockey. Back home from Minnesota for a few days, he decided to take in some international hockey action at the Metro Centre as Slovakia and the Czech Republic met up for an exhibition game.

FACING PAGE:
Number 87 gets ready to lead his charges onto enemy ice at the Halifax Metro Centre.

SIDNEY FRANCHISE: THE ARRIVAL OF NUMBER 87 TO THE Q

JUNE IS THE MONTH OF RENEWAL IN THE HOCKEY UNIVERSE. OPTIMISM REIGNS SUPREME AS TEAMS PREPARE TO RESTOCK THEIR CLUBS WITH FRESH BLOOD THROUGH THEIR SELECTIONS IN THE ANNUAL ENTRY DRAFT. WHETHER IT BE THE NHL OR THE CHL, THE DRAFT IS AN OPPORTUNITY TO REPLENISH AND REBUILD, AN INVITATION TO WIPE THE SLATE CLEAN AND BEGIN THE PROCESS OF BUILDING A WINNING TEAM OR REMAINING ONE. ALTHOUGH EVERY YEAR'S DRAFT IS GREETED WITH KEEN ANTICIPATION, THE 2003 QUEBEC MAJOR JUNIOR HOCKEY LEAGUE DRAFT TOOK ON ADDED SIGNIFICANCE. THE 2003 FIRST-OVERALL SELECTION WOULD NOT BE SOME TALENTED PLAYER WHO HAD A BETTER-THAN-EVEN SHOT OF MAKING THE ROSTER AND STICKING AROUND FOR THE SEASON; THIS TOP PICK WAS THE MOST TALKED ABOUT TEENAGER SINCE ERIC LINDROS.

Sidney Crosby would make his franchise the hottest ticket in the league, and his league the most talked about circuit in the sport. For most, there would be no suspense in terms of where he would begin his QMJHL career. The Rimouski Oceanic owned the first pick in 2003, and that is where Crosby would play. But as the days and weeks flew by, it occurred to some that maybe something other than the obvious would happen. For those who remembered the draft of 2001, Sidney Crosby's selection by Rimouski was not yet a sure thing!

In June of 2001, the QMJHL was prepared to hold one of the deepest drafts in the league's history. Although it had been assumed for months that the first selection would be Steve Bernier, a scoring machine out of Ste.-Foy, Quebec, a draft-day blockbuster seemed imminent to some observers.

Considering that future Sidney Crosby linemates Marc-Antoine Pouliot and Dany Roussin, along with highly touted NHL prospects Stephen Dixon of Halifax and Danny

Sidney Crosby stops on a dime to elude a Moncton Wildcat defender. Crosby's lower-body strength affords him amazing balance on the blades.

Stewart of Charlottetown, were also available in the draft, it would not have been a complete surprise to see a major deal unfold. Ultimately the Moncton Wildcats, sold on the incredible upside that a Steve Bernier choice offered, settled on the future first-round selection of the San Jose Sharks.

The 2001 experience certainly provided food for thought in 2003. Would Rimouski dare trade away Sidney Crosby in order to secure future first-round draft picks? Would they entertain a four- or five-player package deal that would give them instant depth and a secure shot at making the QMJHL playoffs for a number of years?

On Saturday, June 7, 2003, le Palais des sports in Val-d'Or, Quebec, was filled to capacity as QMJHL president Gilles Courteau began proceedings. Sidney Crosby's eagerly anticipated arrival into the ranks of major junior hockey was about to become reality. On cue, a gentleman settled in easily behind his microphone to make an announcement. Was a trade in the offing, or was Sidney Crosby about to become the newest member of the Rimouski Oceanic?

The Raising of the Oceanic

With a single entry-draft selection of a sixteen-year-old centreman, the Rimouski Oceanic set in motion the redefinition of a franchise and the resurgence of a league. For the Oceanic, the arrival of the peerless Shattuck–St. Mary's grad in June of 2003 meant a hastened escape from the abyss and a return to national junior hockey prominence. For the QMJHL, Sidney Crosby's appearance in the double blue of Rimouski signalled a welcome surge of national and international attention, the likes of which it had never enjoyed before, and changed the dynamic of the circuit in every respect, from league attendance to franchise expansion.

The Rimouski Oceanic's quest for national junior hockey supremacy began in 1995. Having revived the defunct St.-Jean Lynx operation, team management methodically transformed itself into a legitimate contender by the beginning of the new millennium. The Oceanic, led by Prince Edward Island standouts Brad Richards and Thatcher Bell, played an up-tempo style that tended to overwhelm opposing defensive schemes. By the beginning of the 1999–2000 season, Rimouski had its sights squarely set on the city of Halifax and that year's Memorial Cup tournament.

The Oceanic were clearly the class of the QMJHL that season. A record of forty-eight wins and twenty losses along with four ties gave notice that they would be the prohibitive favourites to win the President's Cup, the trophy emblematic of Quebec Major Junior Hockey League superiority. A tough final-series win provided the perfect dress rehearsal for a Memorial Cup that saw the Oceanic go through the week-long tournament undefeated. In the final against Barrie of the Ontario Hockey League (OHL), Rimouski easily manhandled the Colts and strode to a 6–2 title-game victory.

In less than a decade of operation, the Rimouski Oceanic, through a combination of shrewd draft picks and sound management, had risen to the top of the junior hockey heap. Rimouski's rise to the national junior hockey summit was thoroughly impressive, but success would come at a hefty price, and the team would soon find itself struggling to escape the second division.

In the years following the win in Halifax, Rimouski's fortunes took a nosedive. Heavily dependent on senior players during their suc-

Quick FACTS

Sidney Crosby led Rimouski, which had missed the 2003 playoffs, back to the post-season in 2004. Following a quarterfinal win over Shawinigan, the Moncton Wildcats ended Sidney Crosby's rookie playoff run.

Sidney Crosby was one very rich teenager. Reebok signed the then-eighteen-year-old professional hockey player to a lucrative multi-year deal.

An all-around athletic talent, Sidney Crosby won an Atlantic Canadian baseball championship with the Cole Harbour Cardinals in 1998.

Sidney Crosby shakes off a check and awaits a feed from a linemate.

The Dynamic Duo. Marc-Antoine Pouliot and Sidney Crosby were probably the most explosive tandem in the QMJHL in 2004–2005.

cessful Memorial Cup run, the eventual graduation and departure of experienced leaders such as Richards (to the Tampa Bay Lightning), Juraj Kolnik (to the N.Y. Islanders), and goalie Sébastien Caron (to the Pittsburgh Penguins) left a chasm in the Rimouski lineup that raw rookie draft picks could not fill. Just three years after their national championship win, the Oceanic sat last in the QMJHL standings.

In 2002–2003, the Rimouski Oceanic managed a paltry 25 points in seventy-two games. The team's eleven wins were the worst in team history, and their sixteenth-place finish in the association was one worse than their previous low. For the first time in their existence, they were forced to watch the post-season festivities from the sidelines.

Despite their humbling bout with adversity, Rimouski garnered little sympathy from CHL rivals. Ironically, it would have been easy to understand if teams had actually been envious of Rimouski's fall. While some CHL organizations struggle in obscurity and mediocrity for decades, just three years removed from a national championship, the Oceanic were about to welcome an all-world talent to their roster. Rimouski was about to become the sole ben-

eficiary of a once-in-a-lifetime talent. Those experts who predicted that Crosby's impact would be immediate and immeasurable could not have been more correct.

From the moment Crosby arrived at camp in August of 2003, the fortunes of the Rimouski Oceanic hockey club rose. The fan base in the hockey-mad town had been thoroughly reignited once again, and the on-ice product had been given instant credibility. The great hockey fans in Rimouski, it seemed, had welcomed number 87 with open arms.

The relationship between Crosby and his mates also seemed to be very good. Teammates admired him and his abilities, while coaches lauded his team-first attitude. Eric Neilson recalls the impression Crosby made: "The first game I ever saw him play, me and [teammate] Mark Tobin were in the stands watching him get point after point. Toby looked over at me and said, 'Darryl Sittler [Leafs Hall of Famer] right there'" (The Crosby Connection).

While it is obvious that Sidney Crosby understood that the expectations in Rimouski were sky-high,

a comment he made following his selection by the Nics put everything into perspective: "Scoring goals and making plays is part of my job. I didn't come with any expectations prior to the season. I'm playing hockey, I'm having fun, and I enjoy it" (The Crosby Connection).

Sidney Crosby's rookie season of 2003–2004 was smashing. It seemed that every game featured an exciting third period come-from-behind win, or another record-breaking performance before another sellout crowd. The storybook season kept getting bigger and better, reaching its crescendo with a dramatic midwinter spectacle in the province's capital.

On a brisk February night in 2004, Sidney Crosby and the Rimouski Oceanic rolled into town to take on the beloved Remparts. With great expectations, 15,333 rabid Remparts fans packed le Colisée to see their team welcome their provincial rivals. It was the kind of attendance figure normally reserved for NHL arenas, and it was an unmistakable sign that Sidney Crosby had a special aura about him. Like Gretzky or Lemieux, Crosby drew capacity crowds regardless of the standings, regardless of the schedule. He alone was worth the price of admission, and that put him in very select company indeed.

Riding the coattails of Sidney Crosby's smashing 54-goal, 81-assist freshman season, the Oceanic climbed ten spots in league standings, finishing with 76 points and adding well over twenty games to the win column. In addition, they enjoyed a return to playoff action, emerging victorious from a quarterfinal-round battle with Shawinigan, only to be subdued eventually by the Moncton Wildcats. As great as the 2003–2004 season was, Sidney Crosby and the Rimouski Oceanic would be even better the next year.

In the 2004–2005 season, the Oceanic secured forty-five wins, including an amazing second-half record that assured the club its best regular season ever. Sidney Crosby, assisted by his talented linemates Dany Roussin and Marc-Antoine Pouliot, played like a man on a mission. "Sidney was just incredible in these playoffs," says Acadie-Bathurst coach Mario Durocher. "The kid was just unstoppable."

Despite Crosby's appearance in the World Junior Championship, which forced him to miss some league games, the dynamic power forward put up brilliant numbers: 66 goals and 102 assists for 168 points placed him first in league scoring and secured his credentials as the CHL's top player for the second year in a row.

As good as the regular season was for both the fans and for Sidney Crosby, the 2005 QMJHL playoff run was even more spectacular and proved once again that in pressure situations, Sidney Crosby seemed to be able to dig down and find another level to

Quick FACTS

In a Memorial Cup semifinal game that will be talked about for some time, number 87 scored three goals and two assists to lead his Rimouski Oceanic team to a 7–4 decision over the Ottawa 67's.

Sidney Crosby reportedly rejected an offer of $7.5 million over three years to sign with Hamilton of the World Hockey Association.

Out of the Kelowna Rockets, the London Knights, the Ottawa 67's, and the Calgary Hitmen, the only CHL club that did not face Sidney Crosby in the 2005 Memorial Cup is the Calgary Hitmen.

Classic Crosby. One of Sidney Crosby's greatest traits as a player is his attention to detail. Here he drives to the net with his stick on the ice and his eyes locked on the puck.

nents, each with their own set of intangibles that the Oceanic needed to address. In fact, Rimouski's first opponent, the Lewiston MAINEiacs, buoyed by an impressive first-round upset over the favoured Shawinigan Cataractes, felt their club might just be primed to derail the mighty Oceanic train before it ever really got rolling.

The Lewiston MAINEiacs had finished the 2004–2005 campaign in fourth place in the Eastern Division, some 26 points behind Rimouski. At first glance the series looked very one sided. The season series saw the Oceanic take three games of four against the U.S.-based club, with many of those not as close as the scores indicated. Still, there were some X factors that seemed to give the MAINEiacs more than a fighting chance against Rimouski. To begin with, Lewiston enjoyed momentum coming off the series with the Cataractes, while Rimouski had gone more than a week without game-day competition. In addition, Lewiston was led by a talented duo capable of engineering an upset of this magnitude. Columbus Blue Jackets draft pick Alexandre Picard and New York Rangers blue-line prospect Jonathan Paiement gave the MAINEiacs a solid one-two punch that Rimouski needed to counter.

his play. Game after game, round after round, he got stronger, more dominant, and more determined. With his leadership skills at the forefront, Crosby consistently willed his teammates to better playoff performances. In order, Lewiston, Chicoutimi, and Halifax fell by the wayside as Crosby and company, with surgical precision, cut through opposition defences and shifted their high-powered offence into overdrive.

The Oceanic's stunning playoff stats do not tell the whole story, though. Each series saw Rimouski have to battle tooth and nail to subdue oppo-

In addition to having some bona fide talent on their roster, Lewiston enjoyed the luxury of no expectations. While Rimouski was expected to win easily over its American counterpart, the MAINEiacs were not expected to go far. Rimouski coach Doris Labonte feared as much, no doubt aware that Lewiston could play with reckless abandon. The MAINEiacs had little to lose as the 2005 QMJHL playoffs began, and that made them very dangerous.

Any suggestion that Lewiston might be intimidated by beginning the series in the raucous Colisée de Rimouski was summarily dismissed by the third period. Benefiting from a needless Rimouski penalty, Lewiston's Alexandre Picard continued his dynamite playoff effort by blasting a shot past Rimouski keeper Cédrick Desjardins. The marker gave the 2005 QMJHL's Cinderella story a 3–2 lead with less than twenty minutes to play.

It seemed that the Rimouski Oceanic were already facing the defining moment in their 2005 playoff run. A Lewiston opening-game victory might just give the underdog the confidence it needed to pull the upset off. In the minutes that followed Picard's go-ahead marker, the Oceanic would have to answer one question: Were they a contender or a pretender? It didn't take long for Crosby and company to decide it was time for the clock to strike midnight on Cinderella.

Beginning with a crucial counter by Danny Stewart, the Oceanic scored four consecutive third period goals on their opponents. Lewiston goalie Jaroslav Halak could not shut down Rimouski's high-powered scoring machine. The Oceanic had dodged a bullet as the top seed rebounded to take the game 6–3.

The eruption of offence in the final frame of game one appeared to change the whole complexion of the series. Opening-game jitters were replaced by confidence and self-assuredness in

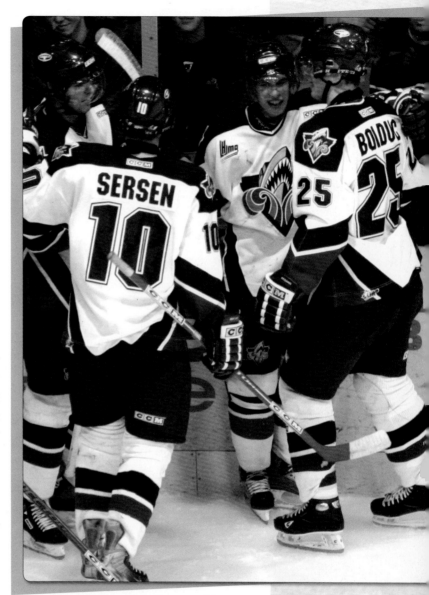

games two, three, and four. The Oceanic's strut had reappeared, and that spelled doom for coach Clément Jodoin and his Lewiston club.

In the previous three games, a combination of outstanding goaltending by Edmundston, New Brunswick, native Cédrick Desjardins and back-to-back-to-back monster performances by

Sidney Crosby accepts congratulations from teammates after scoring a crucial third-period marker against the Wildcats.

Sidney Crosby helped lift the Oceanic to a series sweep over the American upstarts. Crosby, more focused since his quiet opening-game effort, scored 11 points in his next three matches. If Crosby's quarterfinal effort against Lewiston was impressive, his play against Rimouski's semifinal-round opponent Chicoutimi Sagueneens was otherworldly.

In a five-game pounding of their Eastern Division rivals, the Oceanic outscored Chicoutimi 26–9. A number of sensational efforts from different Rimouski players highlighted the Oceanic effort. Once again, Sidney Crosby's effort stood tallest as he tallied 7 goals and 7 assists in the semifinal series. The dominating team performance featured an 11-goal outbreak in game two.

While the Rimouski Oceanic had impressed everyone with their superior play, losing only one game on their way to the finals, another team was also raising eyebrows. The Halifax Mooseheads were overwhelming opponents on their way to securing a spot in the league championship series. It seemed like the perfect scenario: Sidney Crosby would return to his hometown to help his Oceanic battle the Mooseheads for league laurels. The plots and subplots seemed like something out of the Stratford Festival.

Had Hollywood been commissioned to script the 2005 QMJHL playoffs, it would have loved the premise of the prodigal son, this time as a sworn enemy, returning to his native city to do battle. As unlikely as it might have seemed at the beginning of the season, Sidney Crosby's return to Nova Scotia to fight for the right to move on to the Memorial Cup would make for great cinema; it made for even greater hockey.

With the rehearsals over, the big show got underway in Rimouski on Thursday, May 5, 2005. Halifax, having come off a thrilling six-game semifinal victory over Baie-Comeau, featured a swarming attack led by world junior bronze medallist Petr Vrana of the Czech Republic and a stifling team defence that had held post-season opponents to a minuscule 12 goals. Of course, the Mooseheads had not faced a forward unit quite like that of Dany Roussin, Marc-Antoine Pouliot, and Sidney Crosby.

If there was any doubt about just how powerful this Rimouski team was, it was removed early in game one. Against a well-balanced and well-coached Halifax club, the Oceanic scored five first period goals en route to an easy 9–4 opening-game victory. Despite being outshot forty-two to thirty-nine in the match, Rimouski once again displayed an opportunistic offence that pounced on defensive-zone mistakes. Sidney Crosby finished the game with a goal and two assists as he and his teammates set the tone for the rest of the series.

Perhaps the "Hawk" sign to Sidney Crosby's right says it all, as he prepares to pounce on a loose puck.

In game two, Halifax would be forced to step up its offence and thwart Rimouski's run-and-gun style in order to have a shot. A win in game two and the Mooseheads would claim home ice advantage as they headed back to the friendly confines of the Metro Centre for games three and four.

Fighting back with a determination that characterized their season, the Mooseheads erased a two-goal second period deficit to tie the game on consecutive goals by Vrana. The comeback was inspirational, but try as they might, Halifax could not get on top of the Oceanic. A game-winning final-stanza marker by Zbynek Hrdel sealed Halifax's fate, and Rimouski took a 2–0 series lead that they would never relinquish.

Although the Mooseheads never quit for one second during games three and four, it must have become obvious to them at some point that this Rimouski Oceanic team just had too many weapons. As Mario Durocher points out, "Having come this far, Sidney Crosby and his mates were not going to be denied a trip to the 2005 Memorial Cup."

As Yogi Berra might say, game three was déjà vu all over again. Rimouski got off to a quick 4–0 first period lead and never looked back, holding on for a 5–4 victory and a commanding 3–0 series lead.

In game four, the Oceanic continued their pattern of huge second periods as they rode a four-goal middle frame to a series-ending 4–3 win. Although the series featured a couple of one-goal victories, the sweep seemed to be indicative of the advantage in play.

Finishing his QMJHL career in the Nova Scotia capital seemed appropriate. Game four allowed Sidney Crosby to bid a fond farewell to a city that had witnessed the evolution of his career. Crosby would bid adieu to the city of Halifax with one of the finest playoff performances in QMJHL history. His 31 points in thirteen games put him in select company among those few who have won the regular season and playoff scoring race in the same year. How proud the city must have been.

With the junior hockey season drawing to a close, Sidney Crosby's dream of donning the jersey of a professional hockey team was near. But first, Sidney Crosby had some unfinished business that would take him to the southern Ontario city of London and the fitting conclusion to his major junior hockey career.

A New Era for the QMJHL

While Sidney Crosby's arrival ignited the resurgence of a former champion to its rightful place among the CHL's elite teams, it also signalled the beginning of a new era for the Quebec Major Junior Hockey League. Arguably, the least recognized of the three CHL entities before Crosby's selection in the June draft of 2003, the QMJHL stepped out of the shadows afterwards and overtook the Ontario Hockey League (OHL) and Western Hockey League (WHL) as the most important junior hockey league in the nation.

Sidney Crosby's role in the revitalization was key. Perhaps no junior hockey player before him has had such a positive influence on his respective league. Since number 87's arrival in "the Q," his influence in the areas of league attendance, increased national and international exposure, and perhaps most importantly expansion cannot be overstated.

One glance at the attendance figures the year before Sidney Crosby arrived (2002–2003) compared with those of his freshman year gives a pretty accurate picture. In 2002–2003, the Quebec Major Junior Hockey League saw 170,509 patrons rush through its turnstiles. The following year, as the Crosby Caravan trekked across Quebec and the Maritime Provinces, 43,023 more spectators bought tickets. It was a new record for the Q, besting that of the 1999–2000 season. "It was unbelievable," notes Sylvain Couturier, a former L.A. King. "Teams that had been struggling to sell tickets were suddenly seeing standing room only crowds.... It was really something to see how he was bringing fans back to the rinks."

In addition to being a hit with fans, Sidney Crosby, and by extension the league itself, became the focus of intense scrutiny by national and international media alike. The QMJHL, long since a hit with Quebec-based television and radio outlets,

REGULAR SEASON STATS

Team	GP	G	A	P	PIM	+/−
2003–2004 Rimouski	59	54	81	135	74	49
2004–2005 Rimouski	62	66	102	168	84	78

PLAYOFF STATS

Team	GP	G	A	P	PIM	+/−
2003–2004 Rimouski	9	7	9	16	13	5
2004–2005 Rimouski	13	14	17	31	16	11
Memorial Cup Rimouski	5	6	5	11	6	7

THERE ARE NO TICKETS AVAILABLE FOR TONIGHTS GAME JANUARY 18, 2004

A sign of the times. Sidney Crosby and the Rimouski Oceanic sell out the Molson Coliseum during a January 2004 road trip to the Hub City.

began to attract much attention from networks outside the provincial boundaries.

The thirst that sports television networks and print media had for anything Crosby seemingly could not be quenched. Half-hour television sports magazines were beginning "Crosby Watch" segments, and the previous night's efforts by number 87 and his Rimouski Oceanic teammates were often the leading story in morning sports recaps. Box-score summaries in national daily newspapers throughout the nation detailed the Oceanic's every move.

Whether it be through radio or television or the exploding number of Web sites dedicated to teams or players associated with the Quebec Major Junior Hockey League, the Q had suddenly become extremely hip. For the first time, the QMJHL had become larger than either of its CHL brethren. Considering the struggles of the league only a generation before, the Q's comeback, thanks in large part to Sidney Crosby, was truly grand.

Last but certainly not least, Sidney Crosby's influence on league expansion, as subtle as it might have been, was substantial. Just before Christmas 2004, the QMJHL announced the awarding of

FACING PAGE: Sidney Crosby accepts a pass from a teammate during a 2005 game against the Moncton Wildcats.

franchises to two of Atlantic Canada's largest cities, St. John's, Newfoundland, and Saint John, New Brunswick. Each of the Atlantic Canadian entries was able to raise the $3 million needed to join the Q. What was extremely intriguing about that franchise fee is that only months before, the Everett Silvertips were able to enter the CHL for a paltry $2 million stipend. The $1 million spike in bid gives an actual dollar-to-dollar account of just how much Crosby's amazing two-year stint in Rimouski helped increase the value of the league—and the game—in the eyes of prospective owners.

The league's successful move into every corner of Atlantic Canada in 2004 concluded a flurry of recent QMJHL expansion and relocation deals that saw the Q grow from sixteen to eighteen hockey clubs, including seven in Atlantic Canada and one in the United States, based in Lewiston, Maine. The QMJHL had suddenly become the template that select hockey leagues throughout North America copied in the tough world of amateur and professional sport. Rival leagues had taken notice that, both in the boardroom and on the ice, the Q had acquired a sort of Midas touch. Its list of successes is noteworthy.

Each and every one of its franchises is financially secure and looking forward to the 2005–2006 season. The league has teams now in every province east of Ontario, and its future south of the border is secure as well. The Q will once again host the Memorial Cup in 2006. Moncton will follow Quebec City and Halifax as the latest QMJHL city to have such an honour. Record attendance numbers, soaring league revenues … the good news just keeps on coming.

On the ice, the QMJHL is sending impact players to the NHL like never before. The past two Conn Smythe Trophy winners (Brad Richards and Jean-Sébastien Giguère) plus the 2004 World Cup of Hockey MVP (Vincent Lecavalier) are league grads. The Q has participated in the last five Memorial Cup finals and should make it six next year considering they will have two of the four teams at the tournament. The Quebec Major Junior Hockey League has fully recovered from its on-ice malaise of the 1980s and early 1990s and is at the forefront of grooming professional hockey players. QMJHL brass will argue that the arrival of Sidney Crosby was a gift from the hockey heavens. As Acadie-Bathurst Titan administrator Earl Dimitroff states, "The QMJHL will be feeling the benefits of Crosby's presence for a very long time. There is no doubt that the presence of Sidney Crosby in our league in the past few years has rekindled the passion of major junior hockey to our fans."

LEARNING TO LEAD: THE 2004 AND 2005 WORLD JUNIOR CHAMPIONSHIPS

ON JANUARY 4, 2005, SIDNEY CROSBY STEPPED OUT FROM THE SHADOW OF RUSSIA'S ALEXANDER OVECHKIN TO BECOME THE BEST JUNIOR HOCKEY PLAYER IN THE WORLD. ON THAT JANUARY NIGHT IN GRAND FORKS, NORTH DAKOTA, AN INSPIRED CROSBY LED TEAM CANADA TO A GOLD MEDAL WIN OVER ARCH-RIVAL RUSSIA, OUTPLAYING OVECHKIN IN THE MOST ANTICIPATED ONE-ON-ONE BATTLE IN THE HISTORY OF THE TOURNAMENT.

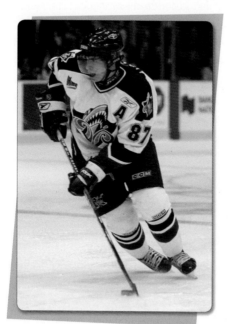

Playing alongside Boston Bruins' rookie sensation Patrice Bergeron and London's Corey Perry, Sidney Crosby played perhaps the most complete hockey of his life. Using a combination of brute strength, balance, and finesse, the Rimouski power forward out-played his Russian rival in every category, leaving little doubt that he had replaced the Moscow Dynamo star as the most talented player in his age group. *Inspired* may indeed be the word that best describes Crosby's effort that evening. From the drop of the puck to his final shift, Crosby displayed the edge, ferocity, and focus that had become the trademark of his game. And while Alexander Ovechkin—who did not play the entire game, leaving in the second period with a shoulder injury—was named top forward in the tournament and named to the tournament all-star team, all eyes were on Crosby.

For the Rimouski forward, this superior performance had been some time in the making. Less than a year earlier, the two top prospects had landed in Helsinki, Finland, for the 2004 World Junior Championship, with Crosby enduring one of the more disappointing moments in his young hockey life.

In January of 2004, a sixteen-year-old Sidney Crosby found himself in the Finnish capital as a member of Team

ABOVE: Sidney Crosby is strong on the stick as he engages an opponent during a QMJHL regular season game in 2004.

BELOW: All championship clubs have at least one thing in common—team chemistry. Here the Oceanic celebrate a playoff goal against Halifax en masse.

team suffer a bizarre and heart-wrenching 4–3 championship-game loss to Team USA.

Crosby's rookie performance in Helsinki had been a far cry from Ovechkin's World Junior Championship debut in Halifax in 2003. As a seventeen-year-old centreman from Moscow Dynamo, Ovechkin was among the tournament leaders in scoring, and he played an integral role in his country's gold medal victory.

It can often be true that some of our greatest accomplishments are born out of profound disappointment. As much as the 2004 World Junior Championship must have hurt Sidney Crosby, it may have ultimately provided the inspiration and motivation for his greatest moment in the sport. From the time he returned from Europe, his game was simply superb. Despite already owning NHL-calibre skills, the Rimouski star seemed intent on getting even better at every facet of the game.

In addition to his superlative natural skills, Crosby seemed determined to bring his natural leadership abilities to the forefront. Former Team Canada coach Mario Durocher had an opportunity to see those skills first-hand: "Sidney's teammates instinctively follow his lead," says Durocher. "Sidney leads by example and in the dressing room, and I think that in 2005 he

Canada. The 2004 World Junior Championship would provide him his first genuine opportunity to show the hockey establishment that he belonged in the same company as Alexander Ovechkin, the Russian star who had taken a "leave" from the Russian Elite League to showcase his tremendous skills to the world. Even at sixteen, the talented Crosby seemed primed to challenge Ovechkin's domination of the junior game.

However, as the tournament progressed, it became clear that Sidney Crosby was not yet ready for prime time. Relegated to playing a supporting role, Sidney Crosby failed to put up big numbers. In four round-robin games in which Canada scored an impressive total of 25 goals, Crosby could muster only 3 points. In the semifinal and final games against the Czech Republic and the United States respectively, Crosby contributed only a couple of assists and watched his

Sidney Crosby gets set to tap in a perfect feed from linemate Patrice Bergeron. Canada defeated the Czech Republic 3–1 to advance to the finals against Russia in the 2005 World Junior Hockey Championship.

wanted to highlight that role." Sidney Crosby seemed comfortable in his role as a calming influence in the dressing room, and as the initial selection camp for the 2005 World Junior Championship grew near, his game was at or near its peak.

At the national team's evaluation camp in July 2005, Team Canada brass instantly recognized the key role the Cole Harbour native would need to play. As a sixteen-year-old, Crosby had come to the final selection camp perhaps willing to take a secondary role in order to make the cut. In 2005, as a returning national team veteran fresh off a spectacular junior season—one that

included winning the CHL's top player award— Crosby would be given a starring role and a spot on the top line.

Throughout the 2005 pre-tournament and round-robin schedule, Crosby's performance was nothing less than spectacular. Having completely put to rest his struggles in Helsinki, Crosby went to work in Grand Forks, racking up eight points on the strength of six goals and two assists. He had put Team Canada on his shoulders and was determined to help carry it into the medal round.

Team Canada defenders team up to stop a Czech Republic
forward from advancing into the Team Canada zone.

Of course, the round-robin portion of the tournament meant relatively little to Team Canada. Since the moment the schedule had been released, the only date on the calendar that held any meaning was January 4, 2005—the championship final. Somehow Crosby must have known deep down that on that date, he and Ovechkin would tangle for the very last time in their amateur careers, with more than just the championship of the world on the line.

2005 World Junior Final

January 4, 2005, Grand Forks, North Dakota
For Sidney Crosby, the night was not about scoring goals and racking up points. No one had ever questioned his ability to put points on the board. It was understood by most that this world junior final was about leadership and the ability to carry a team to a championship. Team Canada would need to put together a sixty-minute effort. Each period of the game would present new and different challenges, and each period saw Sidney Crosby appear to take on a different yet equally important role.

In the first twenty minutes, Crosby played the role of the intimidator. Team Russia, rightfully concerned about the Crosby line's ability to break open a game, was consumed with stopping him and his linemates (Roussin and Pouliot), so much so that other Team Canada forward units seemed to be able to penetrate Russia's zone at will. While Russia used its best defensive forwards to try and contain the Crosby trio, talented Team Canada skaters such as Mike Richards, Ryan Getzlaf, and Danny Syvret consistently broke through to create scoring opportunities.

In the second frame, Crosby's killer instinct came to the fore as he helped set up the scoring play that for all intents and purposes put away the Russians. Crosby, who had been dangerous the entire game but had not yet registered a point, connected with Perry and finally Bergeron on a marvellous three-way

Quick FACTS

Sidney Crosby scored an impressive 14 points in two world junior hockey championships (2004, 2005). The all-time leading point getter in the tournament is his idol, Peter Forsberg of Sweden. Sidney Crosby would like to be able to follow in the footsteps of the Philadelphia Flyers forward. The Olympic gold medallist and two-time Stanley Cup champion combines physical play with impeccable skill … certainly sounds a lot like Crosby's game, doesn't it?

ABOVE: A disappointed Sidney Crosby watches Team USA celebrate their gold medal victory over Canada in the 2004 World Junior Hockey Championship.

passing play to give Team Canada an insurmountable 5–1 lead.

In the final period, Crosby's 2004 world junior experience was put to use as he helped calm and reassure his anxious teammates. It is important to remember that in recent years, Team Canada had become notorious for finding ways to lose. In Halifax in 2003, the home team came into the third period with the game under control and a 2–1 lead, only to have Ovechkin and Team Russia wrestle the lead away en route to a 3–2 gold medal victory.

In 2004, in perhaps the most disappointing game in our nation's junior hockey history, Team Canada enjoyed a 3–1 lead entering the third period of the gold medal match. Head coach Mario Durocher had his team playing superbly, and the overwhelmed Americans seemed to be going through the motions when suddenly the momentum swung inexplicably. Team Canada gave up three unanswered goals in the final twenty minutes to allow Team USA to steal the gold medal with a 4–3 come-from-behind win.

In 2005, Sidney Crosby and his mates were not about to let that happen.

In the final period in Grand Forks, Crosby could be seen talking constantly to teammates, giving directives and encouragement. Right up until the final siren, Crosby was directing traffic, refusing to allow teammates to lose their focus or celebrate too early. As the final seconds ticked off the clock, junior hockey fans around the world knew they had witnessed something very special. Team Canada had proved they were the best … and Sidney Crosby had surged past the Russian rebel to become hockey's best teenage player.

Anyone using the next day's newspaper box score to get his or her sole take on the game might have seen Crosby's lone assist and presumed he'd had an uneventful evening. Nothing could be further from the truth. Sidney Crosby played a complete sixty minutes; he had been everything coach Brent Sutter had hoped for.

Of course January 4, 2005, was significant for Sidney Crosby not only in terms of his rivalry with Alexander Ovechkin; it also marked the night that Sidney Crosby locked in his status as professional hockey's next icon. "No doubt about it. Sidney Crosby's performance at the championships solidified his status as the NHL's next superstar in waiting," says Shattuck—St. Mary's director of hockey operations, J. P. Parisé.

It had become apparent during the 2005 World Junior Championship that Sidney Crosby's leadership skills had become as much a part of his game as his on-ice skills. After watching him perform in Grand Forks, the suits at NHL headquarters must have realized they had finally found that great young talent who possessed

the personal strength, desire, and skill set to become the unquestioned leader of the game.

Since his amazing stint at Shattuck—St. Mary's in 2002–2003, many had hoped that Sidney Crosby could be groomed as Mario Lemieux's heir. On the strength of his performance at the world juniors, Sidney Crosby proved he had the ability to take the lead among NHL superstars as the sport was about to take dead aim once again at the lucrative American and European markets.

FACING PAGE: Sidney Crosby straddles the blue line in a 2003 World Junior game against Switzerland.

BELOW: A Team USA forward moves around Team Canada's Sidney Crosby in the final of the 2004 World Junior Hockey Championship in Helsinki, Finland.

A record-setting marker. With this December 2003 game against Switzerland, Sidney Crosby became the youngest person ever to play in the World Junior Hockey Championship.

In the past decade, a steady stream of young can't-miss prospects have failed to pick up the baton and run with it. Eric Lindros, Paul Kariya, Joe Thornton … all have been stars in their own right, but none appear to have the mass appeal or intrinsic leadership qualities needed to propel the game to the next level. Sidney Crosby does.

The eighteen-year-old has proved over and over again that he has the ability to take a singular sporting event and make it larger than life. He did

it in Bathurst in 2002 at the Air Canada Cup; he did it again at the 2005 world juniors in Grand Forks. The last time the United States hosted the tournament—in 1996—the locals gave a collective yawn and ignored the championship to a large degree. In 2005, the tournament was a ratings winner, due in large part to Crosby's ability to captivate his audience.

NHL brass must have been ecstatic to see how Crosby helped put the game of hockey back on

the front page. The NHL, embroiled in a lockout with the National Hockey League Players' Association (NHLPA), had long since been forgotten by many North American sports fans. Sidney Crosby, with an appeal that stretched across gender and demographic lines, helped put the game squarely back in the limelight with his performance in North Dakota. As the NHL finally resumes play, it knows it has in its midst a player with the ability, through his play and his presence, to bring fans back to the game.

By the way, if anyone had still entertained any doubts about Crosby's ability to make the game a special event, he or she need only look at the 2005 Memorial Cup in London, Ontario. Midway through the week, the CBC did a feature on how big the 2005 tournament had become nationwide. The Memorial Cup, usually seen as a major event only in the host city, had become a national spectacle. Of course, one of the first players mentioned in the piece was number 87 of the Rimouski Oceanic. Sidney Crosby had helped make the 2005 Memorial Cup one of the most widely watched in its history.

Filling hockey arenas is not new to Sidney Crosby. The Quebec Major Junior Hockey League set attendance records in 2004–2005. Each and every arena that Crosby set foot in saw an increase when Sid the Kid came to town. In Quebec City in February of 2004, 15,000-plus came to see the phenom at le Colisée—a perfect illustration of the star power Crosby had attained.

Further proof of Crosby's appeal to the business sector is seen in the giant deal he recently signed

TOP: Sidney Crosby and Patrice Bergeron prepare to accept their gold medals following Canada's 6–1 title-match victory over Russia.

MIDDLE: The best line ever? Canada's top forward unit of Patrice Bergeron, Sidney Crosby, and Corey Perry hoisting the Maple Leaf. The victory in Grand Forks was the first for Canada since 1997.

BOTTOM: The pride of Atlantic Canada. Nova Scotia native sons Stephen Dixon and Sidney Crosby proudly display their silver medals from the 2004 World Junior Hockey Championship.

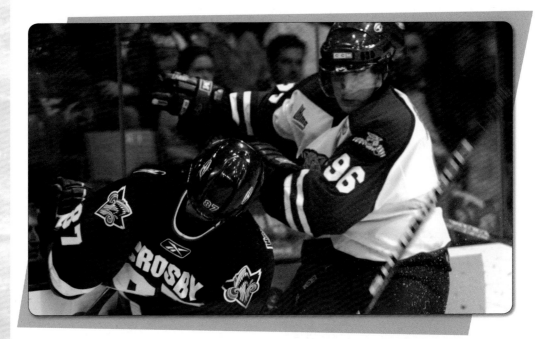

FACING PAGE: Sidney Crosby draws an Ottawa defender into taking a penalty at the 2005 Memorial Cup in London, Ontario. The Oceanic, and particularly Sidney Crosby, were lethal with the man advantage throughout the tournament.

ABOVE: Sidney Crosby gets the worst of a collision with a Moncton Wildcats forward.

BELOW: Sidney Crosby shows his defensive zone posture as the Oceanic line up for a faceoff in front of their keeper.

with Reebok. Reports suggest it is a multi-million-dollar pact spread over five years. One of the more gainful contracts signed in years by a professional athlete, it begins the process of putting Sidney Crosby in the company of commercial endorsement giants LeBron James and Tiger Woods.

Certainly, the 2005 World Junior Championship will be recognized at some point in the future as a watermark for both Sidney Crosby and the sport of professional hockey. For Crosby, the ability to lead, perhaps the most underestimated of all his traits, came to the forefront in Grand Forks in dramatic fashion, and he became a complete player. "For Sidney Crosby, the 2005 World Junior Championship may be remembered as the initial moment he placed himself in the company of Howe, Richard, Gretzky, and Mario," notes J. P. Parisé.

With the NHL entry draft scheduled to take place later that year, NHL owners and general managers came away from the tournament fully aware that the 2005 lottery would offer as its prize one of the most complete hockey players to come into its ranks in the history of the event.

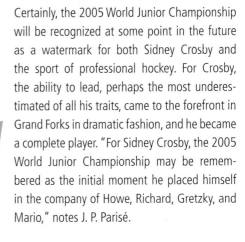

LESSONS IN DEFEAT: THE 2005 MEMORIAL CUP

THE SIGN OF A TRUE CHAMPION IS ABILITY TO APPLY LESSONS LEARNED IN DEFEAT. GETTING BLANKED 4–0 BY THE LONDON KNIGHTS IN THE 2005 MEMORIAL CUP FINAL WAS PROBABLY NOT HOW SIDNEY CROSBY ENVISIONED FINISHING HIS REMARKABLE CHL CAREER, BUT THE LOSS PROVIDED A VALUABLE LESSON, ONE HE WILL TAKE WITH HIM AS HE EMBARKS ON HIS PROFESSIONAL CAREER.

The final match was the only blemish for Crosby in an otherwise superb Memorial Cup. Sidney Crosby's performance, highlighted by a sensational semifinal effort against Ottawa, was one of the strongest in the series. Ultimately, the championship came down to a showdown between the best player in the CHL and the best team in the CHL. This time, it would prove to be London's moment of glory.

London Calling

The 2004–2005 season was perhaps the most successful season in the history of the CHL. Two teams in particular

dominated the sports headlines from beginning to end; the Rimouski Oceanic and London Knights battled each other tooth and nail the entire season for the number one ranking. The 2005 Memorial Cup tournament would settle the debate as to which team was superior.

Even before the drop of the puck, many felt that this national junior hockey championship, hosted by the OHL's London Knights, would be hailed as an instant classic. Few could remember a tournament where so many great players dotted the rosters of

RIGHT: The Rimouski Oceanic, led by their captain Marc-Antoine Pouliot, take their traditional post-game parade around the ice following their final-game triumph over the Halifax Mooseheads. The victory was especially sweet considering the team had been only two years removed from a last-place regular season finish.

TOP: Sidney Crosby's QMJHL career ends on a winning note that included the Guy Lafleur MVP Trophy.

No Memorial Cup could boast having four teams with this much depth and talent. The London Knights, holder of the CHL record for most consecutive games undefeated, sported a 100-point regular season. The Q representative, the Rimouski Oceanic, lost only one game in their dominating playoff run and featured the best line in all of junior hockey.

The Kelowna Rockets, defending WHL and Memorial Cup champions, were relegated to third-seed status in the tournament, giving testament to just how deep this championship pool really was. Last but certainly not least, the Ottawa 67's, who were seen as sizable underdogs in London, had been up against similar odds in their last trip to the final in 1999, only to win the event in a thrilling overtime title-game victory over the Calgary Hitmen.

With all due respect to both the defending champs and the upstart 67's, hockey fans across Canada could not conceal their desire to see London and Rimouski settle the question of which CHL club was superior. Having turned their attention away from the NHL while the pro circuit dealt with its collective bargaining situation, hockey fans nationwide had become caught up in the exploits of these two brilliant clubs. From the beginning of the 2004–2005 season, London and Rimouski had taken turns being the dominating force in junior hockey. It seemed the only definitive way to end the debate was to have them play each other on the national stage. It was an exciting prospect.

the respective CHL champions. Sidney Crosby, the best Canadian Hockey League player two years running, was leading a Rimouski Oceanic club that included snipers Marc-Antoine Pouliot and Dany Roussin. The host London Knights were stacked with future NHL prospects Robbie Schremp, Dan Fritsche, and Corey Perry, while the defending Memorial Cup champion, the Kelowna Rockets, featured potential future Norris Trophy winner Shea Weber and gifted playmaker Blake Comeau.

On Saturday, May 21, 2005, the Memorial Cup opened with a match that had the feel of a seventh game of a Stanley Cup final. London and Rimouski would kick off the tournament with a contest many felt would be a championship-tilt preview. For the Rimouski Oceanic, the key to their success against London in the opener was quite simple. Their best players needed to step up as they had throughout the QMJHL playoffs. The CPR line (Crosby, Pouliot, Roussin) needed to score goals five on five, and the Oceanic power play, a key to their success throughout the season, needed to connect when given the opportunity. Crosby and company knew that the Knights, coached by former NHL legend Dale Hunter, would attempt to make number 87 a non-issue. Somehow Crosby would have to play through the heavy hitting and constant attention and make his presence felt.

The pro-London crowd barely had time to sit down before an unlikely hero brought them to their feet again. Marc Methot, a solid stay-at-home defenceman, picked up a clearing pass at the 2:37 mark and deposited a wrist shot behind a startled Cédrick Desjardins. It would be the beginning of an unforgettable night for the London rearguard.

While the Knights did a good job early on in controlling the Oceanic's top player, the CHL's leading scorer eventually found his stride. His finesse game hindered by an aggressive London double team, Sidney Crosby turned to his amazing power game to get the Oceanic rolling. Taking advantage of a Methot interference call at 6:12, the lethal Oceanic power play went to work. In typical fashion, Crosby withstood a pounding in front of the London net and banged in a rebound to tie the affair at one.

As the first period wore on, it was apparent that London's defence corps was not strong enough to curtail Crosby's awesome cycle game; number 87 repeatedly took the puck down low, feeding his linemates for point-blank scoring opportunities. On the strength of Sidney Crosby's efforts and the play of the Oceanic special teams, Rimouski enjoyed a two-goal lead after the first period. It looked as if the QMJHL representative might run away with the contest. However, the London Knights were unlike any opposition Rimouski had faced all season. Teams from the Q might have wilted under the overwhelming pressure the Oceanic offence was exerting, but the Knights were a worthy opponent—and they had some offensive firepower of their own.

After retiring to the dressing room and making adjustments designed to slow Crosby and the relentless Oceanic attack, the Knights mounted a counterattack of their own. Danny Fritsche, Team USA veteran and NHL blue-chip prospect, began the comeback with a timely marker early in the middle frame. The tide was slowly but noticeably changing in the Knights' favour, and at the 4:02 mark of the third, Anaheim Mighty Ducks draft pick Corey Perry broke through with

Quick FACTS

Mario Durocher, Sidney Crosby's Team Canada head coach in 2004, has an Atlantic Canada connection. After a successful stint behind the bench of the Lewiston MAINEiacs, Durocher was installed as the newest bench boss of the Acadie-Bathurst Titan of the QMJHL in the fall of 2004.

ABOVE TOP: Adam Blanchette of the Moncton Wildcats tries to block Sidney Crosby during an October 31, 2004, match. Crosby scored two goals and an assist in the game, but the Wildcats would eventually prevail by a score of 9–5.

ABOVE BOTTOM: Sidney Crosby attempts to deflect the puck past Moncton Wildcat goaltender Corey Crawford. Crawford and Crosby may soon renew their acquaintance at the NHL level. Crosby, of course, is the first-overall pick of the Penguins while Crawford is a second-round selection of the Chicago Blackhawks.

his first of the tournament to even the match at three.

As the extra session got underway, it was clear that it was just a matter of time before the Knights would break through. At 9:36 of overtime, Methot ended the best game of his career by depositing a sweet feed from Perry after the winger had successfully pulled keeper Desjardins out of position. "It was unbelievable. Corey made a beautiful pass right across the slot," said the eighteen-year-old Methot. "I saw the goalie cheating over to Corey's side. I just shot it as high as I could on him and it went in" (SLAM! sports).

Sidney Crosby and the Oceanic were stung by the game-one collapse. After a league playoff that saw them barely break a sweat on their way to winning the President's Cup, the loss to the Knights had already placed Crosby and company in a bit of trouble. The QMJHL champ could not afford another loss, and there would be little time to make the required adjustments as the gritty Ottawa 67's hockey club waited in the wings.

Two things must have become obvious to the Oceanic as they prepared to play for their playoff lives: If they were to reach Sunday's final, two very important lessons from their opening-game loss

needed to be acknowledged. First, after blowing a two-goal lead to London, it was obvious to some that their defensive game and their goal-tending were not strong enough to protect a lead. Rimouski would therefore need to hold the pedal to the metal on offence and win games by scoring a lot of goals. Second, for the Oceanic to win the rest of their games, a must considering their 4–3 loss to London, Sidney Crosby would need to play an even bigger role in their success than first thought.

From the drop of the puck in their game against Ottawa, it appeared both lessons had been taken to heart. Having been denied on a glorious scoring opportunity just seconds into the contest, Crosby shrewdly used his strength to buy time and space in front of the Ottawa net before one-timing a pass from Oceanic captain Marc-Antoine Pouliot past 67's keeper Danny Battochio at the 11:18 mark.

After the Oceanic and 67's traded goals late in the first period, Sidney Crosby helped Rimouski regain its two-goal lead by engineering one of the prettiest plays in the tournament. In the opening minute of play in the second, Crosby, defenceman Patrick Coulombe, and Pouliot combined on a slick three-way passing play, with Pouliot depositing Coulombe's feed into the back of the Ottawa net.

The 67's would ultimately come back and make a game of it, but Dany Roussin's goal at the

> *THEY PLAYED KIND OF PHYSICAL AGAINST US BUT WE STILL WORKED HARD TO CRASH THE NET AND TRY TO MAKE THINGS HAPPEN.*

7:00 mark of the third proved to be the game winner, securing the Oceanic's first win and a spot in Friday's tiebreaker. "We just tried to move the puck and use our speed—that's what we have to do," said Crosby, who tied Corey Perry of the London Knights for the tournament scoring lead with four points in two games. "They played kind of physical against us but we still worked hard to crash the net and try to make things happen" (SLAM! sports).

The win against Ottawa was the perfect cap on a day that saw Crosby rewarded with the CHL's top honour. The Rimouski Oceanic star took home the league's top individual award—the Reebok CHL Player of the Year. Crosby, who led the CHL with 66 goals and 168 points in sixty-two regular season games, became the first player in CHL history to win the trophy twice. He was also player of the year as a sixteen-year-old in 2004. "It's special for sure," Crosby said. "I just came into the season wanting to improve but at the same time I didn't want to put pressure on myself to win it again. For sure it's special to win it two years in a row" (SLAM! sports). Crosby also took home the CGC Sheet-rock Top Scorer award and the Canada Post Cup three-stars award.

As special and as eventful as the day was for Crosby and his teammates, once again there would be little time to enjoy the moment. Rimouski was right back on the ice the next day in a critical match that would see the Oceanic attempt to eliminate the defending champion Kelowna Rockets.

The situation for Kelowna was dire. Round-robin losses to Ottawa and London meant the Rockets could not afford a defeat at the hands of the QMJHL entry. For Rimouski, a victory would send them directly into Saturday's semifinal match and earn them a valuable day off on Friday.

Determined to avoid a scenario that would see them play three games in three days, the Oceanic finally got some welcome offensive contribution from their second line. Zbynek Hrdel, who had been stealthily quiet during the first two games, opened the scoring for Rimouski late in the first period. Hrdel picked up a rebound from a Mario Scalzo Jr. knuckleball and slipped it behind Rocket goaltender Kristofer Westblom.

The match against Kelowna was never really in doubt. Following Hrdel's icebreaker, the Oceanic got goals from Crosby, Scalzo, and François Bolduc to open up a healthy 4–1 lead. Blake Comeau's deuce in the third period put a bit of a scare into the Oceanic, but ultimately the double blue would hang on and take the contest 4–3.

For the first time in the tournament, Rimouski played a complete team game. The Oceanic turned in a terrific game from top to bottom against the WHL champion, getting contributions from every forward and defensive unit as well as top-notch goaltending from a determined Desjardins.

Sidney Crosby plants himself in front of Halifax Moosehead goalkeeper Jason Churchill during game four of the 2005 league finals at the Metro Centre. Crosby and company would sweep the much-anticipated final series in four games.

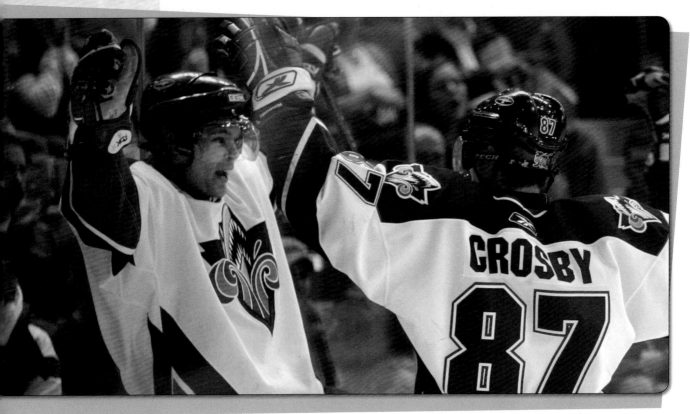

ABOVE: Crosby and his mates join the capacity crowd at the Colisée de Rimouski to celebrate an Oceanic goal.

As was the case in games one and two, Sidney Crosby posted a goal and assist and was terrific at both ends of the ice. For the second time in three games, Crosby was awarded a game-star selection.

With their portion of the round-robin tournament finished, the Rimouski Oceanic had more than forty-eight hours to plan and prepare for their semifinal rematch against the Ottawa 67's. Although still somewhat disappointed that their players had let the opening-round match against London slip through their fingers, the Oceanic brass had to be pleased with the way their team had rebounded, and extremely happy with the performance of their top star.

However, as well as Sidney Crosby had been playing, he had not shown his A game yet. Unfortunately for the Ottawa 67's, Sidney Crosby was about to reach that level with a semifinal game for the ages.

In a game dubbed by some "the Crosby Show," the Cole Harbour native scored three goals and two assists to pace the Oceanic to a 7–4 semifinal win. If ever there was a game that underscored Crosby's killer instinct, it was this one. It seemed that every time the Oceanic needed to fend off the 1999 national champions, Crosby would mastermind another successful scoring drive.

Moncton's Kevin Glode gets the stick up high on Sidney Crosby during a QMJHL regular season game in 2005.

> *CROSBY'S LINE GOT OFF TO A QUICK START IN THE OPENING PERIOD OF GAME 1, AND LONDON KNEW THEY COULD NOT EXPECT TO COME BACK FROM A TWO GOAL DEFICIT AGAIN.*
>
> —Brad Crossley, head coach of the Dartmouth Subways

Quick FACTS

Sidney Crosby will attempt to help keep the Penguins' perfect Stanley Cup–final record intact. The Pittsburgh club is perfect in Stanley Cup–final play, having won their only two appearances in 1991 and 1992.

Crosby opened the scoring for Rimouski less than two minutes into the game and appeared to be a threat to score each and every time he picked up the puck. Whether it be on special teams or five on five, in the offensive or defensive zone, taking faceoffs or playing the wing, Crosby was absolutely dominating.

Number 87 would score a goal in each of the regulation periods, including a floater from centre ice that caught nothing but mesh. The hat trick, in addition to assists on goals by Pouliot and Scalzo, secured Crosby's third game-star selection in four games.

Crosby's play in the semifinal win over Ottawa left many shaking their heads over just how good number 87 was. Just when you thought you had seen the kid do it all, he would come up with a performance like he did in the Memorial Cup and raise the bar even higher. In true Crosby style, however, he was not about to take sole credit for the performance. "We play as a team, we win as a team, we lose as a team," is an earlier Crosby quote that refkects the young man's thoughts following the postgame ceremonies (Crosby Connection).

The Rimouski Oceanic were peaking at just the right time. As difficult as it would be to beat a rested London Knights team the following afternoon, Crosby's performance in the semifinal must have put London on notice that Sidney Crosby was coming into the final firing on all cylinders.

And Then There Were Two

Before the final game, the Knights' coaching staff recognized the importance of denying Rimouski's top line of Crosby, Pouliot, and Roussin. "Crosby's line got off to a quick start in the opening period of game one," notes Brad Crossley, head coach of the Dartmouth Subways, "and London knew they could not expect to come back from a two-goal deficit again." Dale Hunter, seemingly acknowledging the fact that defenceman Daniel Girardi failed to control Crosby in the opener, once again handed the job of neutralizing the tournament's top scorer to power forward Brandon Prust. It was this matchup that very likely would determine the 2005 national junior championship.

The John Labatt Centre was electric as the starting players skated to centre ice for the puck drop. For hockey purists, the rumble between London and Rimouski, two teams that had equal amounts of respect and dislike for each other, was perfect. The number one and two ranked teams in the nation were finally settling the issue … *mano-a-mano*.

In hindsight, the Oceanic probably wished they had handled the opening five-minute stanza better. Eric Neilson and Jean-Sébastien Côté, perhaps too concerned with establishing an early physical presence, picked up consecutive cross-checking infractions to put the Oceanic two men down. Dan Fritsche, the London Knights veteran, continued his strong tournament play as he beat Cedrik Desjardins to open the scoring four minutes into the match.

Unlike previous tournament matches, Sidney Crosby did not get off to a fast start. For the second consecutive meeting, Prust, the six-foot native of London, was doing an effective job of negating the Oceanic superstar. With Crosby struggling to find skating room, the Oceanic's offensive game ground to a standstill, and the Knights began to assert control over the championship game.

Whether it was the fatigue factor (two sudden-death games in less than twenty-four hours) or a case of nerves setting in, the Rimouski Oceanic looked nothing like the well-oiled machine that had steamrolled over Ottawa in the semifinal. By the end of the second period, markers by Bryan Rodney and David Bolland had given the Knights a seemingly insurmountable 3–0 lead.

Despite Doris Labonte's attempts to spring free his superstar, the Oceanic simply did not seem up to the task. The Knights defence,

Sidney Crosby eyes the net as he prepares to blast another powerful shot at an opposing goalie.

51

London's Trevor Kell finds himself in a one-on-one battle with Rimouski's Sidney Crosby during the opening match of the 2005 Memorial Cup. The OHL champion would eventualy subdue the Oceanic 4–3 in the extra-session thriller on a goal by defenceman Marc Methot.

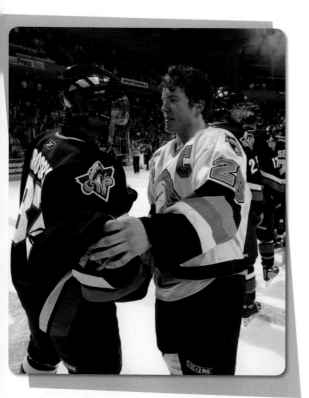

best. London's 4–0 shutout of Rimouski was dominant from start to finish, leaving no doubt that the 2004–2005 edition of the London Knights would go down as one of the truly great teams in CHL history. For the Knights and their fans, their fortieth year in operation would be one not soon forgotten. For starters, London had reeled off a CHL-record thirty-one-game undefeated streak that broke a decades-old mark set by the Brandon Wheat Kings. The 2004–2005 Knights also became the first team in OHL history to record back-to-back fifty-win and 100-point seasons. Most important of all, the London Knights had put an end to a near half-century of drought, bringing home their first-ever national junior title.

For Sidney Crosby, it must have been a devastating loss, perhaps in some respects comparable to the gold medal game defeat at the hands of the Americans in January of 2004. Brandon Prust had done an exemplary job of shadowing Sidney Crosby, perhaps even providing him with an invaluable lesson.

Sidney Crosby is an incredible talent, very aware that in every game he plays as a pro, there will be a Brandon Prust waiting to try and shut him down. Whether it be Kris Draper, Mike Peca, Jere Lehtinen, or John Madden, over the course of his career, number 87 will be hounded game in and game out by the best

which had been seen by some as the team's Achilles heel, had thrown a suffocating blanket over the Oceanic attack. If Rimouski fans had hoped the intermission would help turn the tide, Edmonton Oilers prospect Robbie Schremp quickly put an end to those hopes.

With a final game performance that may have sold Oiler GM Kevin Lowe on his NHL credentials, the Fulton, New York, native Shcremp snapped a wrist shot past Desjardins early in the third, signalling the end of the night for Desjardins.

As the seconds wound down on the season, it was apparent that the London Knights had bluntly ended the debate as to which team was Canada's

Quick FACTS

In January of 2004, World Cup of Hockey MVP Vincent Lecavalier lost his Rimouski rookie goal-scoring record to Sidney Crosby when number 87 of the Oceanic scored his forty-third goal of the season in a 4–1 loss to Chicoutimi.

In July of 2005, Sidney Crosby joined a select group of QMJHL alumni who were picked first overall in the NHL draft. Pierre Turgeon, Alexandre Daigle, and Vincent Lecavalier are just a few from the Q to be so honoured.

London Knight captain Danny Syvret, number 25, and Sidney Crosby, number 87, exchange best wishes following the Knights' Memorial Cup clinching win. Syvret and Crosby were both part of the national junior team that won gold in Grand Forks, North Dakota, in January of 2005.

RIGHT: Sidney Crosby fields questions during a Rimouski Oceanic post-game show. Number 87 has always had a reputation for being one of the more approachable athletes in the game of hockey.

FACING PAGE: The home of Troy and Trina Crosby in Cole Harbour, NS, was a popular destination for the media as they tried to garner reaction to the NHL lottery held in July 2005. Pittsburgh bested Anaheim and won the right to select Crosby first overall.

> *THE CHAMPIONSHIP GAME ASIDE, NUMBER 87'S PERFORMANCE AT THE MEMORIAL CUP WAS NOTHING LESS THAN BRILLIANT.*

checkers in the world—and he will need to overcome it. There is no doubt that being shut out in the Memorial Cup championship game was not how the young man wanted to end his junior hockey career, but the lessons learned from the experience may truly end up being priceless.

The championship game aside, number 87's performance at the Memorial Cup was nothing less than brilliant. Sidney Crosby's 6 goals and 5 assists for 11 points in five games led the tournament, earning him the Ed Chynoweth Trophy for top scorer. Crosby, along with teammate Mario Scalzo Jr., also earned first-team all-star status. In a tournament filled with memorable performances, Crosby's accomplishments and high level of play were unequalled. Truth be told, the Rimouski Oceanic would not have advanced to the Memorial Cup had it not been for number 87. He made a good team great, and in the

process showed NHL owners why the kid is worth his weight in gold.

For the Canadian Hockey League, the Memorial Cup final of 2005 marked the end of an era. Sidney Crosby, recognizing that it was time to fulfill a dream, bid adieu to the Quebec Major Junior Hockey League and prepared to step into the arena of professional hockey.

7

THE ROOKIE

SIDNEY CROSBY ARRIVED IN PITTSBURGH ARMED WITH SUCH AN ACCOMPLISHED HOCKEY RESUMÉ THAT HE WAS CONSIDERED A FRANCHISE CORNERSTONE, CAPABLE OF ELEVATING THE PENGUINS' TO A LEVEL OF SUCCESS NOT WITNESSED SINCE THE TEAM WON BACK-TO-BACK STANLEY CUP TITLES IN THE EARLY 1990S.

Only eighteen years of age at the start of his first NHL season, Crosby was already a world-class athlete, possessing the physical gifts and personality traits that set him apart from his peers. He scored 120 goals and 183 assists in 121 games over two seasons in the QMJHL and was named Canada's Major Junior Player of the Year in both seasons. While most hockey observers predicted he would be an impact player as a rookie, Crosby said publicly (and modestly) on many occasions that his top priority was just to make the Penguins roster. "I'm looking at it as short-term as possible. I want to have a good camp and push myself to raise my game as best I can," Crosby said. "Obviously,

this is a new level, but the pressure has always been there. I've always put a lot of pressure on myself to perform."

With number 87 coming to town, the Penguins went to work improving the rest of their roster. Forward Mark Recchi, who first played for the Penguins from 1988–92, re-signed with Pittsburgh as a free agent after the 2003–04 season. Soon, he was joined by defencemen Sergei Gonchar and Lyle Odelein, forwards Ziggy Palffy and John LeClair, and goaltender Jocelyn Thibault. "Playing with those guys is great, but practicing is where you are really going to benefit, just by seeing their habits," said Crosby. "It's going to help me.

The 2005–2006 Pittsburgh Penguins were a mix of proven veterans and exciting new prospects. In this picture Mark Recchi sits with the Pens' number-one pick.

As for the team, to have that many guys come in, to sign that many guys is just a great situation for everyone." These new players, including Crosby, the young centrepiece, were part of a plan to re-launch the franchise— to make the team competitive again and help it reconnect with its dwindling fan base. (In 2003–04, the team averaged 11,877 fans a game, lowest in the league.)

Following a short summer off-season, Crosby moved in with Penguins owner and captain Mario Lemieux, who had suggested the arrangement after the entry draft. After only a few days at his new home, Crosby knew his living situation was going to be a great learning experience. "I've been talking to him a lot to learn little things," said Crosby. "He's got a great family. It's a good environment for me to be in. I'm just trying to learn as much as I can."

If there was one player in the league that Crosby could learn from, it was Lemieux. Like Crosby, Lemieux came to the NHL after dominating the QMJHL. In two hundred regular season games with the Laval Voisins from 1981–84, Lemieux had scored 562 points. He knew the pressures, the media requirements, and understood that

The mentor and the student. Sidney Crosby will have the added benefit of playing and living with the legendary Mario Lemieux in his inaugural season in the NHL.

Crosby has faced intense media scrutiny from a young age.

Penguins were suddenly the media's main focus, and Crosby's first training camp was truly an unprecedented spectacle. All four Canadian sports channels—TSN, The Score, RDS, and Sportsnet—had crews on location for extensive coverage. In some cases, reporters filed more than one story a day and broadcasted live for network supper-hour shows appearing north of the border. Four major Canadian newspapers—the Montreal *Gazette*, *Toronto Star* and *Sun*, and *Globe and Mail*—sent reporters to Pittsburgh to cover the camp.

The *Globe and Mail*, sensing that Crosby would not be a fleeting storyline, even assigned reporter Shawna Richer to the team for the entire regular season so she could document his every shift. Richer accumulated such a treasure trove of Crosby information that she later wove the entire season into a bestselling biography, *The Rookie: A Season with Sidney Crosby and the New NHL*.

Crosby would benefit from a more sheltered off-ice environment while dealing with the scrutiny. "I got some attention but not like he's getting," said Lemieux, as he reflected on his own rookie season more than two decades ago. "Especially in Canada and especially here in Pittsburgh."

Training camp for the Pittsburgh Penguins 2005–06 season began on September 16, 2005. Crosby skated in the morning on-ice session alongside his new teammates. After the morning skate, in a jam-packed media room at Pittsburgh's Mellon Arena, Crosby talked about his long-awaited arrival in the NHL. "I was a little nervous. Obviously this is my first NHL camp, my first time skating with all those guys all at once," said Crosby. "Once I got on the ice and started playing I settled down pretty easily."

A small market team that had finished last in the thirty-team NHL before the lockout, the

Taking all the attention in stride, Crosby fit in quickly with his new team. On October 8, 2005—three days after their debut against the Devils—the Penguins kicked off their home schedule against the Boston Bruins, and Crosby scored the first goal of his NHL career. Considering his flare for the dramatic, Crosby's first goal was fairly underwhelming, the result of a not-so-spectacular goalmouth scramble. With 1:16 to go in a Penguins power play and his team clinging to a 5–4 lead, Mark Recchi dumped a loose puck toward the net. When goaltender Hannu Toivonen's sprawling kick save sent the puck to his left, Crosby was there to score into a wide open net, giving Pittsburgh a two-goal lead and the opening night crowd something to cheer about. Crosby finished the game with a goal and two assists, but the Penguins lost 7–6 in overtime. After the game, Crosby lamented the Penguins' loss more than he celebrated his first-ever goal. "It's something you dream about, scoring in the NHL," Crosby said. "There's a lot of emotion that comes out of that. But it would have been nice if we had finished it off."

While Crosby's career was off to a solid start, the Penguins soon discovered they were not as strong as team captain Mario Lemieux predicted during the preseason. The Penguins did not win their first game of the season until October 27, a 7–5 topping of the Atlanta Thrashers. The start would prove to be portentous, as the Penguins were on their way to having the second-worst

record in the NHL. Despite their struggles, the Penguins and Crosby did enjoy a few bright spots. The first one came on November 10 in Crosby's first game against the Montreal Canadiens, the team he cheered for growing up in Cole Harbour.

Pittsburgh opened the scoring on a Crosby power play goal at 7:01 of the first period and Lemieux made it 2–0 eleven minutes later. But the Canadiens rallied. Craig Rivet closed the gap to 2–1 late in the second period, and Christopher Higgins tied it at two with just 3:31 to go in the third period, forcing overtime. It appeared Montreal would emerge with the come-from-behind victory, out-shooting the Penguins 6–2 in the extra period. But former Canadien Jocelyn Thibault came through with several game-saving stops for the Penguins, and the game headed to a shootout. Michael

Being shadowed by some of the best checkers in the NHL is nothing new for Sidney Crosby. Pictured here in Crosby's first NHL game in New Jersey is Jay Pandolfo of the Devils, given the task of shadowing the league's top pick on this night.

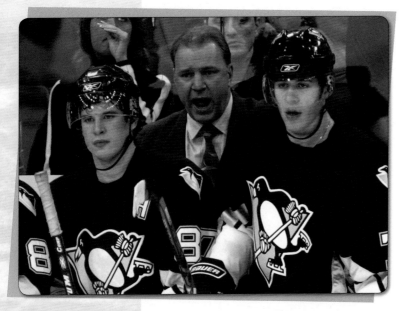

One of new head coach Michel Therrien's first moves was to make Sidney Crosby an assistant captain.

the ice with him," Mario Lemieux said. "He just came out with a great play on that shot."

Another big moment filled with even more intense media pressure came two weeks later on home ice against the Washington Capitals, a team that featured fellow rookie Alexander Ovechkin. Two years older than Crosby, Ovechkin had been drafted first overall by the Capitals in 2004—one year before Crosby—and was already a rookie sensation in his own right. The duo's exciting style of play was already drawing comparisons to another high-scoring NHL pair, Wayne Gretzky and Mario Lemieux. Speaking with reporters the day before the game against Washington, Crosby downplayed the Gretzky-Lemieux comparisons. "We played twenty games or twenty-one games, so to compare us to Mario and Gretzky is a little early," said Crosby. "I think that we have a lot to prove before we can put ourselves at that level."

Ryder, Mark Recchi, Alexei Kovalev, Mario Lemieux, and Alexander Perezhogin all failed to score, leaving the final opportunity of the first round to Sidney Crosby. With his father in the stands, 16,254 fans standing and cheering, and several hundred thousand more watching the game in Canada on TSN, Crosby broke in from centre ice. He kicked his leg, deked Montreal goalie Jose Theodore, and flipped the puck into the meshing at the top of the net, sending Theodore's water bottle into the air.

The goal was a spectacular play, and the Penguins celebrated as if they had just won a championship. After the game, Crosby acknowledged that defeating the team he worshipped as a child was one of the bigger thrills of his young career. "It's so amazing, it's hard to believe," Crosby said. "I was just fortunate to get that shot. I got lucky with that shot." His captain also weighed in, discussing the poise the eighteen-year-old displayed in a pressure-packed moment. "He's quite amazing. It's great to be on

Both players were living up to preseason expectations. Crosby, less than two months into his rookie campaign, was on pace for a 98-point season. If Ovechkin maintained his scoring pace, he would finish the season with 62 goals. Although both had helped energize the NHL fan base in the aftermath of the cancelled 2004–05 season, the two players employed widely different styles of play. Crosby was a fleet-footed finesse player who excelled with incredible on-ice vision and playmaking. Oveckin possessed those attributes, but he played a more physical game and scored more goals than Crosby did.

But other comparisons between the two were mostly unfavorable for Crosby. While Ovechkin was receiving a lot of good press for goals and punishing hits, not all of the media attention directed at Crosby was positive. In several games, including a home-and-home series against cross-state rival Philadelphia, Crosby was accused of being a diver—a player who drops to the ice in an attempt to draw a penalty against the opposition. The strongest accusation came from Flyers head coach Ken Hitchcock. "But that's just 'Hitch' being 'Hitch,'" said Crosby's teammate Mark Recchi, suggesting Hitchcock was merely trying to distract Crosby. "That's fine. We all know [Crosby] doesn't. If you can get an edge against a rival you do it."

All of these distractions and media reports were coming together at once to create a dramatic setting for Crosby and Ovechkin. Dozens of reporters from across North America were on hand to cover the game. "For me I have to approach it like another game," said Crosby following the pre-game skate. "Obviously there's a lot of excitement around it. I'm up for it." The game itself was close, a 5–4 Penguins victory. As for the individual showdown, Crosby narrowly outperformed his rival by scoring a goal and adding an assist, while Ovechkin registered one assist.

Even with Crosby and the other off-season additions, the 2005–06 Pittsburgh Penguins were not a very good hockey team. In fact, they were performing almost as badly as they had prior to the NHL lockout. By mid-December the team had a dismal 8–17–6 record, and general manager Craig Patrick decided to make a change. Patrick fired head coach Ed Olczyk and replaced him with former Montreal Canadiens head coach Michel Therrien. "The team had shown its face and, for whatever reason, they weren't listening," said Patrick. "We look pretty on paper but what are we? What are we? I don't know, but we're going to find out."

What the Penguins quickly found out was that under Therrien, more changes were in the works. The first major shift in how the team would look involved the naming of Crosby as Penguins assistant captain. "This is a new beginning for our team. And [Crosby] is one of our best players," Therrien said. As for the notion that putting an "A" on an eighteen-year-old's jersey was too much pressure, Therrien responded by pointing out that Crosby brought leadership qualities that belied his age. "I don't think it's pressure," said Therrien. "He's a young kid, but sometimes a young kid has good, new ideas."

Not everyone agreed with Therrien. Continuing a criticism of Crosby that dated back to his days with Rimouski, *Hockey Night in Canada* commentator Don Cherry was quick to find

Calder Memorial Trophy

Team Canada assistant captain Sidney Crosby takes the puck up the ice in the
2006 world hockey championships.

fault with the move. When asked by co-host Ron MacLean to comment on Crosby's assistant captaincy, Cherry blasted Therrien, and then Crosby. "Therrien makes the kid an assistant? Please," said Cherry. "Come on, that's ridiculous. I almost gagged when I heard about it. No kid should have as much to say as he's got to say. Yapping at the referees, doing the whole thing, golden boy."

In the end, the move didn't make much of a difference—the Penguins remained mired in a dismal season. Another blow to the organization came on January 25, 2006, when Mario Lemieux announced his final retirement from the NHL. At age forty, and having suffered through a multitude of injuries—as well as cancer—throughout his career, the Penguins captain/owner had been diagnosed with an irregular heartbeat. Rather than risk his health any further, Lemieux decided to end his playing career. "This is always a difficult decision to make for any athlete," said Lemieux. "I feel the time has come. It is in the best interest of me, my family, and the Pittsburgh Penguins."

Reaction from around the league was unanimous in praising Lemieux for his on-ice accomplishments and overall contribution to hockey. The moment was also filled with symbolism—a passing of the torch from the previous generation to the newer and younger talent that had entered the NHL. Wayne Gretzky acknowledged that factor within hours of Lemieux's announcement. "The good news is we've got some good, young players, like Crosby and Ovechkin, come along," said Gretzky. "So I'm sure they'll carry the torch."

Sidney Crosby's rookie season was, by any measure, a tremendous success. After being left off Canada's roster at the 2006 Turin Winter Olympics, he enjoyed a two-week break at home in Cole Harbour and then rejoined the Penguins to finish the season on a torrid scoring pace. On April 17, 2006, in the Penguins' second-last regular season game, Crosby recorded three assists to help lift his team to a 6–1 victory over the New York Islanders. The three points lifted Crosby to the 100-point threshold, making him the youngest player in NHL history to reach the mark, and only the second eighteen-year-old (Dale Hawerchuck was the first).

The next night the Penguins finished the regular season in Toronto with a 5–3 loss to the Maple Leafs. Crosby scored his 39th goal of the season and recorded his 63rd assist to finish his rookie season with 102 points. "One hundred points would be one [of the highlights]," Crosby said of his rookie year. "After the Olympic break it was a lot of fun playing with this group. We weren't winning as much, but I can't see other teams in the same situation reacting the way we did." The two points on the final night of the season also broke Mario Lemieux's team record of 100 points by a rookie set in 1984–85. "It's an accomplishment, for sure," Crosby said. "Just to be mentioned with him is an honour."

As the Pens' season ended, Crosby took advantage of the chance to wear the maple leaf once more, playing on Canada's entry at the 2006

Ovechkin's Rookie Status

Alexander Ovechkin entered the NHL as a twenty-year-old rookie blessed with blazing speed and an incredible shot. In his first career game on October 5, 2005, Ovechkin scored twice against Columbus, serving notice that he would have a tremendous impact in the league. But was he a rookie? Ovechkin had played part of four seasons with the Russian Elite League's Moscow Dynamo, a professional league that paid its players, which by NHL rules would negate Ovechkin's rookie status, and leave him ineligible for the Calder Trophy. But the interpretation of what constitutes a professional league is not an exact formula. For example, the quality of play in the QMJHL is better than some of the lower-level European professional leagues. In the end it was determined, but not without controversy, that Ovechkin was an eligible rookie—paving the way for him to capture the 2005–06 Calder Trophy.

Quick FACT

....

NHL Rookie Qualification

To be considered a rookie, a

player must not have played

in twenty-five or more NHL

games in any preceding

seasons, or in six or more NHL

games in each of any two pre-

ceding seasons. The age of the

player is also a determining

factor. Any player at least

twenty-six years of age by

September 15 of that season

is not considered a rookie.

IIHF men's World Hockey Champion-ship in Riga Latvia. Team Canada, coming off a disappointing finish at the Winter Olympics in Turin, Italy, did not fare much better, even with Crosby. In the preliminary round, Canada went 3–0, outscoring its opponents 14–5. But things went downhill from there: Canada lost in the semifinals to eventual gold medalist Sweden and then faltered in the bronze medal game, losing 5–0 to Finland.

But while his country's performance was subpar, Crosby's was not. Crosby scored eight goals and added eight assists in nine games at the tourna-ment, was named the top forward, and earned a spot on the all-star team. "It's tough to be done with the [NHL] season that early," Crosby said. "It's never fun. I had never really experienced being off that early, so it was great to get more hockey in."

Following the tournament, Crosby returned to Cole Harbour and prepared for the NHL awards presentations in June. Along with Ovechkin and defenceman Dion Phaneuf of the Calgary Flames, Crosby was a finalist for the Calder Trophy as NHL rookie of the year.

Before the regular season began most hockey pundits assumed that Ovechkin had a slight advantage over Crosby because he was two years older and more physically mature. Ovechkin had also played a few seasons for Moscow Dynamo in the Russian Elite League, an experience that was a significant step up from Crosby's two years with Rimouski. Ovechkin, with 106 points to Crosby's 102, did wind up winning the award. "I'm very happy right now," Ovechkin said at the time. "It means a lot."

Although the award results were not in Crosby's favour, the NHL wasn't complaining about the dynamic young forwards. Both Ovechkin and Crosby had produced tremendous campaigns. Both had helped resurrect the National Hockey League just when the game was in peril fol-lowing a year-long lockout. Now the fans had returned in healthy numbers, and the league had two fresh faces to help market the game.

SOPHOMORE SEASON

SIDNEY CROSBY BEGAN HIS SECOND NHL SEASON MUCH THE SAME AS HIS FIRST. EVEN THOUGH MARIO LEMIEUX WAS NO LONGER A TEAMMATE, CROSBY ONCE AGAIN MOVED IN WITH LEMIEUX'S FAMILY AFTER VACATIONING DURING THE SUMMER MONTHS IN COLE HARBOUR.

Behind the scenes the Penguins had made some changes. For starters, long-time general manager Craig Patrick was let go on July 1 when his contract was not renewed after seventeen seasons. "This was a difficult decision we did not take lightly," Penguins president Ken Sawyer said. "But we all agreed it was time to make a change and move forward." Within weeks the organization hired Ray Shero as Patrick's successor. A former assistant general manager with Nashville and Ottawa, the forty-three-year-old Shero was a youthful match for a team coming off a disappointing finish the previous year but still considered a future contender. "Everyone in the hockey world knows about the Penguins' young talent, and the tremendous potential that we have here," said Shero when he accepted the position. "I'm looking forward to working with the players, coaches and staff—and I can't wait to get started."

The 2006–07 Penguins had a different look on the ice as well. Joining the team were two impressive young players ready to make the jump to the NHL—Jordan Staal and Evgeni Malkin. Malkin had been drafted by the Penguins second overall at the 2004 NHL entry draft, but spent three seasons playing for Metallurg Magnitogorsk in the Russian Super League. In a strange turn of events, Malkin was forced to flee his team on a road trip in order to pursue his dream of playing in the NHL. This was the result of a dispute over a transfer agreement between Russian teams and the NHL and Metallurg Magnitogorsk's unwillingness to allow Malkin to leave the team. When Malkin finally arrived in North America, it was yet another piece to the team Shero was building around Sidney Crosby. With the transfer incident now behind him, Malkin could finally look forward to his new career in Pittsburgh. "I've always been very open in my desire to come to North America and be one of the best here," Malkin said through an interpreter. Even though his long-awaited NHL debut was delayed after a preseason shoulder injury, Malkin's rookie season still saw him total 85 points in 78 games and capture the Calder Trophy as the NHL's top rookie.

Craig Patrick, all smiles here as he introduces Sidney Crosby as a Pittsburgh Penguin, was not retained as general manager after Crosby's rookie year.

Jordan Staal's journey to Pittsburgh was less tumultuous, but had just as significant an impact. Just eighteen years old heading into training camp, Staal was thought to be on his way back to the Ontario Junior Hockey League when Shero surprisingly named the 2006 first round draft pick to the Penguins' regular season roster. "Jordan has earned his spot on our roster and deserves to play at the National Hockey League level," Shero said. "We all knew about his skill level when we drafted him, but his work ethic, maturity, and consistent effort have enabled him to make what is normally a difficult transition for a teenager." With Crosby, Staal, Malkin, and a solid mix of veteran players, it appeared, at least on paper, that Pittsburgh

had the potential to be a vastly improved squad from the previous season.

Unlike the previous season when the Penguins did not compete for a playoff spot, 2006–07 was a much different story, as the Penguins went from underachievers to Stanley Cup contenders. On October 19, 2006, the Penguins defeated the New York Islanders 5–4 in overtime on Sergei Gonchar's game-winning goal. The victory evened Pittsburgh's record at three wins and three losses after six games, and the Penguins would not drop below the .500 mark for the rest of the regular season.

On January 13, the Penguins travelled to Philadelphia with an 18–17–7 record. A 5–3 victory over the Flyers started a stunning streak of sixteen games without losing in regulation time. When the streak ended, Pittsburgh was cruising toward a playoff spot with a 32–17–9 record.

Behind the team's improved play was Sidney Crosby. The NHL's leading scorer at the all-star break with 64 points, nineteen-year-old Crosby became the youngest player selected to an All-Star game, garnering the most fan votes (825,783). "It's an honour," Crosby said. "Growing up watching it who would have dreamed of playing in it?" The game was held in Dallas, and Crosby, who played on a line with Ovechkin and Brendan Shanahan, was held pointless as the Eastern Conference lost to the Western Conference 12–9. "You'd think with all the goals scored out there, I'd have been able to get in on one of them," Crosby joked. Even Wayne Gretzky, to whom Crosby was often compared, was held pointless in his first all-star game, a fact Crosby found encouraging when told after the game. "Maybe I'll sleep a little easier tonight," he remarked.

Recent history had been unkind to the Penguins franchise. Between 2001 and 2006, the team had lost seventy-nine games more than it had won. With a playoff berth usually out of reach by early spring, the team would traditionally audition players from the minor leagues and perhaps trade away a high-salaried player for prospects or future draft

The curtain is about to open on another NHL season as parents Troy and Trina Crosby and agent Pat Brisson watch Sidney prepare for his first-ever regular season game against the Devils.

Three of the Penguins first round draft picks from recent years—Sidney Crosby, Marc-André Fleury, and Evgeni Malkin.

was even born. Roberts was a leader, had won a Stanley Cup with the Flames in 1989, and had performed well for the Toronto Maple Leafs in previous playoff appearances. While Roberts had hoped to be traded to an Ontario-based team, he welcomed the move to Pittsburgh and the opportunity to play for a team loaded with young stars that were becoming the talk of the NHL. "He knows that the Penguins are a great young team," said Roberts's agent, Rick Curran. "Rex [Recchi] told him, 'These kids are so great, and they work so hard.' That was music to Gary's ears. He enjoys working with kids who want to work hard and improve."

The other player Shero acquired at the trading deadline was Georges Laraque from the Phoenix Coyotes. A renowned fighter, Laraque gave the Penguins more toughness and provide Crosby with more on-ice protection. Throughout Crosby's rookie season and through the first half of the 2006–07 season, hockey analysts had complained that the Penguins were not doing enough to insulate Crosby from the day-to-day physical abuse that takes place in the NHL. With Laraque in the lineup, the thinking went, it was unlikely that other players would continue to take liberties with number 87. The 2006–07 Penguins had youth, talent, speed, skill, size, and veteran flavour sprinkled throughout the lineup. Now they had much-needed toughness. All of these were considered crucial ingredients for a successful playoff run.

picks. But this year would be different. The team was playing very well. Sidney Crosby was the most popular and arguably the most talented player in the league. General manager Ray Shero decided to shop for players at the trading deadline who could help in the post-season. The first player Shero grabbed was Gary Roberts from the Florida Panthers. At forty, Roberts was old enough to be Crosby's father. In fact, the year Roberts was drafted by the Calgary Flames—1984—was three years before Crosby

But the biggest and most important ingredient, by far, was Sidney Crosby. One year after his breakthrough rookie season, Crosby elevated his performance and quickly established himself as the most exciting player in the NHL. He won the Art Ross Trophy as the league's leading scorer with 120 points (36 goals, 84 assists) in 79 games, six more than runner-up Joe Thornton from the San Jose Sharks. Crosby also became the youngest Art Ross winner ever. Wayne Gretzky was slightly younger when he tied Marcel Dionne for the NHL lead with 137 points in 1979–80 but Dionne had won the trophy for scoring more goals. Crosby also edged out Gretzky by 140 days to become the youngest player to post 200 career points. Crosby finished his sophomore season with 222 career regular season points, reaching 200 at age 19 years and 207 days. He also showed a flair for clutch play by scoring five game-winning goals.

It didn't take long—two seasons in fact—but already Sidney Crosby was excelling in the NHL just as he had in Midget Triple-A, high school, and major junior hockey. His next challenge was the Stanley Cup playoffs.

The Penguins marked their return to the Stanley Cup playoffs with a matchup with the Ottawa Senators in the opening round. Ottawa and Pittsburgh had finished tied during the regular season with 105 points, but the Senators were awarded the higher fourth seed in the overall standings because they had 48 wins to the Penguins' 47. Even though the Senators had home-ice advantage, many expected the Penguins to emerge victorious in the best-of-seven-game series. Pittsburgh had improved

Sidney Crosby and Alexander Ovechkin, two of the NHL's biggest, and youngest, stars, talk to the media at the 2007 all-star game in Dallas.

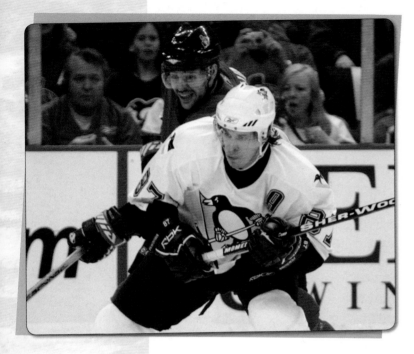

Sidney Crosby looks to corral the puck in a playoff game against the Ottawa Senators in April 2007.

around Crosby was even brighter. Every game was broadcast nationally by *Hockey Night in Canada*, and it seemed even when Ottawa began dominating the series, the television cameras and commentators focused on Crosby more than any other player. Still, Crosby performed well under the conditions, scoring three goals and adding two assists in the five games he played. "It was a big turnaround," explained Crosby. "The playoffs were tough, but maybe it was something that had to happen for us to learn." While disappointed with the outcome, he was already primed for the next season, when expectations would be much higher for the Penguins. "Looking at the big picture, it was a great season," Michel Therrien said. "We have to be optimistic about the future."

As Therrien, Ray Shero, and the Pittsburgh Penguins' players looked to future, they did so with Sidney Crosby leading the way. Already the Pens were "his" team: he was the face of the franchise and by far its best player. Shortly after being eliminated from the playoffs, the team announced Crosby would become the youngest team captain in NHL history. The Penguins had not had a captain since Mario Lemieux announced his retirement in January 2006. "It is obvious to all of us—coaches, players, management, staff—that he has grown into the acknowledged leader of the Pittsburgh Penguins," said Shero. "It is only appropriate that he wears the 'C' as team captain."

dramatically as the season progressed, and expectations were suddenly high for a team that finished 34 points out of a playoff spot just twelve months earlier.

Ottawa was also a team that had steadily improved its performance as the season wound down, but expectations for the Senators were still modest based on previous playoff failures. Ottawa had never had much success in the playoffs, and most hockey pundits were expecting another quick exit. They were wrong.

After splitting the first two games in Ottawa, the Senators won the last three games of the series by a combined score of 9–3, advancing with a four-games-to-one opening-round win. In the playoffs, the intense media pressure

On June 14, 2007, with the Anaheim Ducks still celebrating their Stanley Cup victory, the stars of the National Hockey League gathered in Toronto

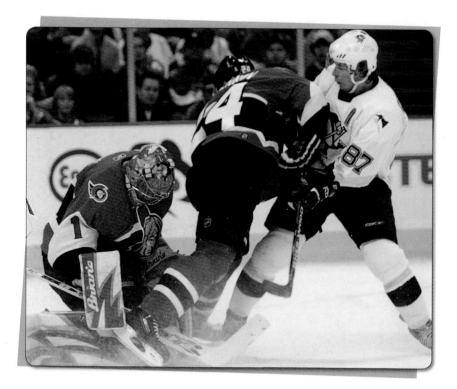

Penguins First Round Draft Picks

The Penguins, through the draft and by way of trade, have in recent years built a stockpile of first round draft picks. Some are young, others are aging veterans. Listed below are the eleven former first round picks that make up the Penguins twenty-two-man roster.

1. Marc-André Fleury (2003)

2. Sidney Crosby (2005)

4. Evgeni Malkin (2004)

5. Jordan Staal (2006)

6. Gary Roberts (1984)

7. Colby Armstrong (2001)

8. Petr Sykora (1995)

9. Sergei Gonchar (1992)

10. Brooks Orpik (2000)

11. Ryan Whitney (2002)

for the league awards ceremony. Several storylines emerged that night, including Martin Brodeur from the New Jersey Devils winning his second consecutive Vezina Trophy as the NHL's top goalie, and Crosby teammate Evgeni Malkin taking home the Calder Trophy. But the night, and most of the hardware, belonged to Sidney Crosby. As the NHL's scoring leader, he was awarded the Art Ross Trophy. He also took home the Pearson Trophy as the NHL's Most Valuable Player, as voted on by members of the National Hockey League's Players' Association.

The evening ended with the presentation of the Hart Trophy as the MVP of the NHL, and again Crosby was called to the podium to accept the honour. It was a record-setting night for the nineteen-year-old, as he became the youngest player ever to win each of these major awards. "The fans love him," Brodeur said. "Everybody seems to be on his wagon, and that's well deserved. He's going to be like Gretzky in making the NHL a better sport."

Just four years after playing for Nova Scotia at the 2003 Canada Winter Games in northern New Brunswick, Crosby was the most famous and arguably the best hockey player in the world. As he accepted the Hart Trophy, Crosby used the moment to thank his parents, sitting in the audience. "The sacrifices of my parents, the early mornings, the practices," Crosby said. "I owe a lot of thanks to them."

ABOVE: Sidney Crosby drives to the net in the 2007 NHL playoffs versus the Ottawa Senators.

It had become clear the Penguins organization owed a lot to Crosby, too. On July 10, 2007, less than a month after the NHL awards presentations, the Pittsburgh Penguins announced they had signed Crosby to a five-year contract extension. The new deal runs through the 2012–13 season and will pay number 87 $43.5 million (U.S.), or an average of $8.7 million per season. "That seems like a pretty good number," Crosby, who was born on the seventh day of the eighth month in the year 1987, said during a press conference announcing the deal. "We

Sid the Kid not only led the Penguins into the NHL playoffs, but also won the league scoring title. Crosby is shown here scoring a shootout goal against Henrik Lundqvist of the New York Rangers.

Record Breaker

It did not take long, but after his second NHL season, Sidney Crosby had set eleven records, either with the NHL or with the Penguins franchise:

1 *Pittsburgh Penguins' franchise record for assists in a season by a rookie*

2 *Pittsburgh Penguins' franchise record for points in a season by a rookie*

3 *First rookie to record 100 points and 100 penalty minutes in a season*

4 *Youngest player in NHL history to record 100 points in a season*

5 *Youngest player in NHL history to record 200 career points*

6 *Youngest player in NHL history to have two consecutive 100-point seasons*

7 *Youngest player to be voted to the NHL All-Star Game*

8 *Youngest player in NHL history to win the Art Ross Trophy*

9 *Youngest player in NHL history to win the Lester B. Pearson Award*

10 *Youngest player in NHL history to be named to the first all-star team*

11 *Youngest player in NHL history to be named a full team captain*

have a lot of young guys and hopefully over the next six years we can all grow together," Crosby told CTV News as he took a break from a training session at the Cole Harbour Place fitness facility. "I think Ray [Shero] has talked a lot about keeping that core together and we've made a lot of steps to do that. It's nice to know I'll be with those guys."

Crosby's fame extended outside the hockey world, too. He had quickly become one of the most recognized celebrities in North America, and his name was aligned with some major corporations. By the time he turned twenty years old, Crosby was endorsing Gatorade and

Reebok, and in August 2007 he released his own line of clothing, a collaboration with Reebok and SportChek. When the line was unveiled in Toronto, Crosby admitted he actually sat down with designers and offered his opinion on certain colours and styles. "It was the last thing I'd imagine myself doing. But we had fun with it." Crosby was also featured on the covers of *GQ*, *Vanity Fair*, and *Time magazines*, and in January 2008 he was number one on the *Hockey News* top 100 list of people of power and influence in hockey, the first time a player, and not an executive, was named to the top spot.

Crosby poses with the three trophies he collected at the NHL awards night in June 2007. Crosby became the youngest NHL player ever to win the Hart Trophy as league MVP.

A new long-term contract, a young competitive team to grow with, a new arena on the horizon, a "C" on his sweater, and a mantel laden with three new major awards. It took just two seasons, but Sidney Crosby and his Penguins were on their way. What at one time was just a promising prospect on a last-place hockey team was now a Gretzky-like superstar on one of the better organizations in the NHL.

Jim Balsillie

For years, even with the presence of Mario Lemieux and then Sidney Crosby, the Penguins were constantly in financial trouble. One reason was Mellon Arena, the oldest rink and lowest revenue generator among NHL buildings. Lemieux had always maintained that in order for the team to survive in Pittsburgh, a new arena had to built. After a deal with a local casino (one that would have included the construction of a new facility) fell through, Lemieux announced the team was officially for sale. In October 2006, billionaire Jim Balsille, the CEO of Research in Motion, announced his intent to purchase the Penguins for $185 million (U.S.). But Balsille made no secret of his intention to move the team to Canada, and when NHL commissioner Gary Bettman told him his impending purchase would have relocation restrictions tied to it, Balsillie backed out. This failed purchase set into a motion a process with the state of Pennsylvania that, in the end, secured a new arena for the Penguins and resulted in Lemieux deciding not to sell the team after all. It was an awkward time for the organization and its players, but it settled the Penguins' fate and secured the franchise's viability in Pittsburgh.

CHASING DESTINY

SIDNEY CROSBY IS ALREADY AMONG THE BEST AND MOST IMPORTANT PLAYERS IN THE HISTORY OF THE NATIONAL HOCKEY LEAGUE. BARRING INJURY, NUMBER 87 MAY EVEN SURPASS THE RECORDS AND ACHIEVEMENTS OF WAYNE GRETZKY TO TAKE HIS PLACE ATOP THE LIST OF THE GREATEST PLAYERS THE GAME HAS EVER PRODUCED. IF SIDNEY CROSBY IS TO USURP "THE GREAT ONE" AS HOCKEY'S BEST EVER, HE WILL NEED TO ACHIEVE THREE THINGS: HE MUST SCORE 3,000 POINTS; HE MUST LEAD HIS TEAM TO STANLEY CUP TITLES; AND LAST, BUT NOT LEAST, HE MUST EQUAL OR SURPASS NUMBER 99'S IMPACT ON THE GAME, NOT JUST BY LEAVING A MARK BUT BY CHANGING THE SPORT ITSELF. THESE THREE ACCOMPLISHMENTS WOULD NOT HAVE BEEN ATTAINABLE HAD SIDNEY CROSBY BEGUN HIS NHL CAREER A DECADE AGO, BUT A FORTUITOUS DRAFT LOTTERY, GROUNDBREAKING RULE CHANGES, AND SIDNEY CROSBY'S OWN STAR QUALITY NOW MAKE THESE GOALS NOT ONLY POSSIBLE BUT PROBABLE.

When Gretzky retired in the spring of 1999, he did so with an impressive all-time-best point total of 2,857. No one has ever reached the 3,000-point mark, but time is on Sidney Crosby's side. As Gretzky did, he joined the NHL as a teenager; two decades into his career, he will still be young enough to be an impact player with the ability to accumulate 100-point seasons.

Sidney Crosby's game is a combination of power and finesse. No player can match Crosby's ability to win with either weapon. He has the slick playmaking ability to go on an end-to-end rush, skating past overwhelmed defenders on his way to faking the goalie and depositing the puck top corner. Or, he can use his lower body strength to run over opposing players on his way to burying one past an equally helpless keeper.

Because he is willing and able to play the game both ways, Sidney Crosby creates unique scoring opportunities. Unlike number 99, who preferred to set up behind the net or on the perimeter to get his goals and assists, Crosby is willing to plant himself in the crease and pick up the tip-ins, rebounds, and garbage goals. In order to play this way, however, a player needs to be able to take the brutal punishment NHL defencemen are more than willing to dish out. Luckily for Sidney Crosby, he has this grit.

Crosby's nose for the net means he has a real shot at breaking some of Wayne Gretzky's scoring records. Here, the Pens' star is about to pounce on a loose puck in a game versus the Toronto Maple Leafs.

Quick
FACT

Pittsburgh hasn't been to the Stanley Cup finals since 1992. That year, Mario Lemieux, Jaromir Jagr, and Ron Francis carried the Pens to a four-game sweep of the Chicago Blackhawks.

There isn't a superlative around that hasn't been used to describe Crosby's game. His skating is better than most NHL players', and his passing ability is finally getting the recognition it deserves. His shot is one of the hardest and most accurate in the NHL. He can take important faceoffs, and he is such a smart player that coaches want him out on the ice in the last minute of important games. Sidney Crosby hits, Sidney Crosby scores, Sidney Crosby leads… and with this talented group of young Penguins, it may be his leadership abilities that become his largest contribution.

Crosby has played in three regular seasons and only a handful of playoff games. He has not even begun to scratch the surface of what will undoubtedly be an incredible professional hockey career, but already the similarities between Crosby and another legendary athlete are unmistakable.

In 1984, a struggling National Basketball Association welcomed a North Carolina Tar Heel by the name of Michael Jordan into the league. Years prior to his arrival, the NBA was a second-division professional sports league struggling to fill its buildings and desperate to find a way into the hearts and minds of basketball fans across North America. From the moment Air Jordan played his first game as a Chicago Bull until he retired from the game in 2003, he was the cornerstone of his sport, and his popularity was the driving force behind the NBA's emergence as a top-four professional sports league with a world-wide popularity that now rivals soccer.

To some, asking Sidney Crosby to do for the NHL what Jordan did for the NBA is asking too much, but Crosby's record of taking the teams and leagues he plays for to greater heights is impec-

cable. He helped take the Dartmouth Subway AAA midget club and make it one of the most noteworthy in the nation; a year later, number 87 took a successful prep-school program at Shattuck–St. Mary's and made it one of the more recognizable hockey programs in the continent. In 2003, Sidney Crosby led a Rimouski Oceanic franchise mired in last place to within one game of a Memorial Cup national championship, in the process making the QMJHL the most talked about league in junior hockey.

Quick FACT

Sidney Crosby is not the only one in his family to get a taste of the NHL. Although he never played a game in "the bigs," Sidney's dad Troy was a twelfth-round selection of the Montreal Canadiens in 1984.

Penguins captain Crosby celebrates a Sergei Gonchar game-winning goal in overtime.

One of the amazing things about professional hockey is that once in a generation it places before us an athlete who reminds us why we love the sport so much. Sidney Crosby is special in the eyes of Canadians because he has the ability to make us recall what it is about the game of hockey that we cherish. As with many things, it will be the journey rather than the destination that is truly important. In a decade's time, we will be able to look back with more certainty and see exactly where Sidney Crosby ranks among the all-time greats of the game, but in the meantime, know that you are watching a remarkably talented young hockey player.

Quick FACT

The NHL came perilously close to losing Sidney Crosby's services for the 2005–2006 season. Having lost an entire season (2004–2005) to a lockout, the league and the players' association had to burn the midnight oil in order to successfully iron out a collective bargaining agreement for the 2005–2006 season.

Photo Credits

Assaff, Peter, 11, 24 bottom

Campbell, Craig/Hockey Hall of Fame, 62

Dahlin, Tom/Hockey Hall of Fame, 1, 17, 18

Dartmouth Heritage Museum, 3

Deschenes, Steve/Hockey Hall of Fame, 54, 58

Dubel Photo Inc., 71 left

Guitard, Flo, 74

Halifax Herald Limited (republished with permission), cover, 7, 9, 13, 20, 21, 41 bottom, 60, 63, 64

MacLellan, Doug/Hockey Hall of Fame, 61

Manor, Matthew/Hockey Hall of Fame, 10, 11, 12, 14

McCaughan Photography, 71 right

Nova Scotia Sports Hall of Fame, 4

Pivovarov, Viktor/Moncton Times & Transcript, 22, 24 top, 26, 27, 29, 31, 33, 42, 46, 48, 49, 51

Polk, Matt/Hockey Hall of Fame, b/c, iv, 55, 59

Sandford, Dave/Hockey Hall of Fame, 35, 36, 37, 38, 39, 40, 41 top, 41 middle, 43, 52, 53

Shattuck–St. Mary's School, 15, 19, 20

CP/Frank Gunn, 75

AP/Gene J. Puskar, 60, 66, 80

CP/Aaron Harris, 78

CP/Jonathan Hayward, 70, 72

AP/Mary Altaffer, 68

Paul Arseneault

Paul Arseneault lives in Belledune, New Brunswick, and is a teacher at the middle school level in the Dalhousie/Campbellton/Bathurst district. He has played and coached a number of sports—including hockey—at the minor, senior/intermediate, and college levels, garnering provincial, Maritime, and national championships. Paul has followed Sidney Crosby's career closely since the early 1990s.

Acknowledgements

First, many thanks to Dan Soucoup and Sandra McIntyre at Nimbus Publishing for giving me the opportunity to write this book, and to everyone at Nimbus for their support. Thanks to Heather Bryan at Nimbus for photo research, designer Troy Cole and editor Patricia MacDonald. I would like to thank the coaches, general managers, administrative staff and journalists who added their expertise to this book. I would also like to acknowledge the efforts of research assistant Tom Moore. Thanks also to Mark for his support.

Paul Hollingsworth

Paul Hollingsworth is a Halifax-based reporter/anchor at CTV Atlantic and a correspondent for SportsCentre, TSN's flagship news and information program. He currently resides in Dartmouth with his wife, Tamara, daughter, Jamieson, and son, Dawson, the namesake of former Montreal Expos centerfielder Andre Dawson.